Gin O'Clock

Extracts from the Royal Diaries

by The Queen*

* of Twitter: @Queen_UK

HO

First published in Great Britain in 2011 by Hodder & Stoughton
An Hachette UK company

First published in paperback in 2012

3

Copyright © @Queen_UK 2011

'Gin O'Clock' is a registered trademark

The right of @Queen_UK to be identified as the Author
of the Work has been asserted by them in accordance with
the Copyright, Designs and Patents Act 1988.

A CIP catalogue record for this title is available from the British Library

ISBN 978 1 444 73976 3

Printed and bound by Clays Ltd, St Ives plc

Hodder & Stoughton policy is to use papers that are natural, renewable
and recyclable products and made from wood grown in sustainable
forests. The logging and manufacturing processes are expected to
conform to the environmental regulations of the country of origin.

Hodder & Stoughton Ltd
338 Euston Road
London NW1 3BH

www.hodder.co.uk

For Queen and Country

Contents

Christmas and New Year at Sandringham

- Wednesday 1st December, 2010
' "Sandringham time" has officially started. Thank God.'

First morning at Sandringham. It is absolutely bloody freezing. One might have thought that someone would have heated the place up. We arrive on the same day every year so it's hardly a surprise. Still, on the bright side, 'Sandringham time' has officially started. This means that sweet sherry may be consumed after 10 a.m. and gin and Dubonnet after midday. There's nothing like a sharp libation to warm up a Queen.

Sent off an email to all government departments reminding them, for the total and unequivocal avoidance of doubt, that this is Christmas. Not 'Festive Time'. Not 'Winterval'. Not 'Seasons Greetings'. Christmas. By Royal Command. Mr Clegg responded by asking what time he was expected at Sandringham. One assured him that he would not be required at Sandringham over Christmas – or approximately ever, for that matter.

Have decided to break with tradition and publish a selection of extracts from the Royal Diaries. Mr Blair's memoirs (filed under 'fiction' or 'humour' – one can never decide) have provided a most useful doorstop in the Royal Library and one thought it about time one's musings saw the light of day.

Mentioned the idea to Mr Cameron. He seemed to take it OK, although did have to rush off to the toilet rather unexpectedly. Must have had a dodgy Custard Cream. The DoE thinks it's a wonderful idea. He has been trying to have his diaries published for years but somehow has never managed to get them cleared by one's solicitors.

Pitched up in the Royal Archives with a large sweet sherry and a tube of Pringles and started to flick through the last couple of years. Best not mention that unfortunate incident that Mr Clegg had at Balmoral. And probably best not to go into the King of Spain's little habit.

• **Thursday 2nd December, 2010**
'Absolutely bloody freezing. Up to one's arse in snow.'

Bacon sandwich and out for a long walk with the corgis. It's like midwinter in Norfolk. Actually, it is midwinter. Poor Linnet the corgi came back with a frostbitten arse. Spent the entire afternoon sitting behind her with a hairdryer, which reminded one to call the Home Secretary and check that she got one's Christmas card.

Julia Gillard, one's Australian PM, called about 3ish. That woman is a total bogan. One does worry for the future of one's Australian people. Seriously considering sending Prince Edward to take personal charge, but he doesn't cope well in the heat.

Wondering about having the Australian population swapped with the French. The DoE says being able to keep a close eye on Gillard and having the French on the other side of the world would be ideal on both counts. Worth some thought. One is still Queen of France, of course, but plays it down for obvious reasons.

• Friday 3rd December, 2010
'The Cabinet Secretary has arrived for his annual audience with his Queen. Taking him for a walk with the corgis.'

Up early and out for a long walk with the Cabinet Secretary, Sir Gus, who has arrived for his annual Christmas Visit. Told him it hardly seems possible that Cameron is still in Government. Even less so that the civil partnership between him and Mr Clegg hasn't ended in divorce. Although there was that affair with Mr Miliband. Still, as Diana used to say, there's three of them in that marriage.

We had a good chat about the general election
farce. He said all was well that ended well. One
asked him what exactly he thought had ended
well and he swiftly changed the subject. How
one's people decide between political parties, one
will never know. They all even look the same.
One really couldn't have faced Mr Brown turning
up every week for five long years. But then look
at what one ended up with. The DoE thinks that
Mr Cameron is some kind of robotic waxwork,
but Sir Gus doesn't think he is that sophisticated.

Sir Gus said he could imagine that a hung parliament
must be a sovereign's nightmare. Told him that the
DoE always thinks a hanged parliament would be
a better solution. Although the uncertainty did get
Charles excited. One had to repeatedly tell him that
he could call whom he liked and it wouldn't have
made a jot of difference.

Apparently, like almost everyone else in Whitehall,
Sir Gus had never met Mr Clegg. Told him that
the DoE had to Google him to find out who he was

and why he was on the news every five minutes. Yes, it all got a bit awkward. It was like one was all of a sudden Queen of Italy or something.

Sir Gus said they came to an agreement as fast as was possible, but quite frankly one has no idea what took them so long. One can distinctly remember spending an evening with a sweet sherry, looking at three corgis – two trying and failing to mate and one chewing its own arse – and couldn't help but draw political comparisons. Finally had to send a message to Mr Clegg to tell him that speed-dating was over and it was time to make a decision. He said he needed a few more Lego bricks to work out the parliamentary arithmetic. Sir Gus said they've come in very handy ever since and that he's almost finished building a red, yellow and blue police station.

Sir Gus apologised again about Mr Brown's episode at the Palace. It all got a bit emotional when he came over to resign; said he wondered if it was too late to take it all back, was confident of being able to form a working majority if he were allowed to involve the Swedish, etc. Finally had to resort to sacking him – although agreed to put 'Resigned' as the reason for leaving on any future job references – and had him escorted off the premises at the end of a bayonet.

And then of course one nearly dialled Cameron Diaz by mistake. In hindsight one wonders if it may have been a better idea.

Popped the Cabinet Secretary back in his car with a packet of Wine Gums for the journey and settled down for an evening of last minute Christmas card writing. Not that they're likely to get delivered this side of Christmas. Bit embarrassed about 'Royal' Mail to be honest.

• SATURDAY 4TH DECEMBER, 2010

'Mr Cameron on the phone. One does wish he wouldn't address one as if one were a public meeting, as Queen Victoria used to say.'

Bacon and mushroom sandwich for breakfast, washed down with a pot of Norfolk tea.

Had Mr Cameron on the phone for a quick 'Queen's Speech'. The DoE said it was more like a 'Queen's Bollocking'. He said he was 'always delighted to discuss matters of state'. Reminded him that one *is* the State, gave him a list of approximately five hundred things to do by Christmas and moved onto Caribbean matters.

Overran slightly ruling Papua New Guinea and was unconstitutionally late for a phone call with the Barbados kiddies. Was so far behind schedule by the end of the day that one completely ran out of time to supremely govern the Church of England. Sent the Archbishop of Canterbury a text to let him know that one would govern him in the morning instead and told him not to make any significant religious decisions in the meantime.

Sadly more film disappointment for Prince Edward. Sacha Baron Cohen has pipped him at the post to play Freddie Mercury in the new Queen film. He's so upset. He'd only just got over not being selected for the lead role in *Dirty Dancing*. He would have been great opposite Patrick Swayze. He spent the rest of the day in a sequinned jumpsuit, singing into a golf club, just to make a point.

Spent the evening with the DoE, a *Poirot* DVD and a tube of Pringles.

- SUNDAY 5TH DECEMBER, 2010
'Phillip, is there anything you wouldn't shoot?'

Spent a quiet day at Sandringham. The DoE popped out to shoot some photographers first thing and came back with a brace of pheasants and several long lens cameras.

Took the corgis out for a long walk after breakfast and found Camilla stuck in a hole. Absolutely no idea how she got down there. One would never have seen her if it weren't for the smoke signals. Finished walking the corgis and pulled her out on the way back.

The DoE spent the rest of the day slaving over an enormous vat of mulled wine ready for Christmas celebrations and Edward iced the cake, as he does every year. Although when the Duchess of York was around she insisted on stirring in the currants, which upset him a bit. Still, he has it all to himself now, although when he's done we do still send the bowl over to her to lick.

Edward takes the Christmas cake making very seriously, or at least as seriously as is possible to in a reindeer outfit. At least we know where he is with that little bell on his hat.

8 p.m.: The afternoon was a bit of a write off, thanks to industrial quantities of Holy Water (gin) after lunch. Woke up in time to find out that one hadn't won the lottery. Again.

• MONDAY 6TH DECEMBER, 2010
'The DoE always thought Jeremy Hunt was rhyming slang.'

Awoke to James Naughtie on Radio 4 getting somewhat tongue tied introducing the Culture,

Media and Sport Minister, Jeremy Hunt. The DoE texted in to say he always thought Jeremy Hunt was rhyming slang anyway. They didn't read it out.

Spent most of the day on the phone to one's Prime Minister in Belize for his annual 'Are you ready to come back under British rule?' appraisal. Despite much pleading, one concluded that they'd have to tough it out on their own until Mr Cameron had got the economy back on track, which could be approximately never, according to Sir Gus.

Apparently there's a shark on the loose in Sharm el Sheikh. Might send the Cabinet off there for a well deserved holiday. It's supposed to be nice at this time of year.

7 p.m.: Settled down in the evening to the special *Coronation Street* tram crash ahead of the Royal *Corrie* Fancy Dress Party. Mr Clegg called halfway through, in a hell of a state.

Managed to stop him crying and assured him that *Coronation Street* isn't real. He seemed to calm down a little and said that he now at least understood why Norris hadn't answered any of his letters.

The Royal *Corrie* Party went swimmingly. Camilla came as Rita, the DoE came as Ken, Andrew as Chesney and Charles as Norris. Anne had made a giant tram out of cardboard boxes and we all stood round while she chucked it off of the top of the stairs. Very lifelike. Although, after a few too many whiskies, the DoE called the fire brigade, who looked a little nonplussed when they arrived.

• TUESDAY 7TH DECEMBER, 2010
'One is not a quango.'

Spent the morning ruling in the Bahamas, where it's nice and sunny and seems to be going broadly according to plan.

Had time before lunch to review Mr Cameron's
latest spending cuts plan. Apparently there's
going to be a 'bonfire of the quangos'. No idea
what a quango is. Asked one's private secretary
to check that one is not one. He confirmed that
one isn't, but suspects that the Prince of Wales
may be.

One's press secretary popped in to say that
Mr Assange and his Wikileaks bunch of merry
men had got hold of a copy of one's diaries
and that there was a danger that the DoE
would be outed as The Stig from *Top Gear*.
Had Assange arrested just in case and poured
a large gin and Dubonnet for reasons of a
diary-security nature. Strictly speaking,
one never indulges in a gin before 5 p.m.
Thankfully it's always after 5 p.m. somewhere
in the Commonwealth.

Spent the afternoon leafing through the rest
of Mr Cameron's proposed spending cuts.
Contrary to recent reports, the DoE has not

been 'cut' in the spending review. Neither, it would seem, has the Prime Minister.

Made a few suggestions for things that could be cut without any impact on the public:

- The Cabinet
- Downing Street
- Chequers Court (Country Retreat of the Prime Minister)
- Carlton Gardens, St James's (Official Residence of the Foreign Secretary)
- Admiralty House (Ministerial Flats for use by Ministers)
- Chevening House (Country Residence of the Foreign Secretary)
- Dorneywood (Country Residence of the Deputy PM)
- Bute House (Official Residence of the Scottish First Minister)
- The Speaker of the House of Commons
- Lord Sugar
- Richard Madeley

- Vanessa Feltz
- Staines
- Channel 5
- Europe

Waiting to hear back.

- **WEDNESDAY 8TH DECEMBER, 2010**
'At Wood Farm with Camilla. It's been very dark since she wallpapered over the light switches.'

Spent the day at Wood Farm, a little cottage on one's Sandringham Estate that the Prince of Wales uses, with Camilla and the corgis. She'd spent the week decorating but has just noticed that she'd wallpapered over the light switches. Said it's not a problem: that's what candles were invented for. Looks rather nice, actually; strong tartan print. The Pope had suggested it when he visited earlier on in the year and she'd taken his advice to the letter.

Actually still recovering from the Papal Visit. His Holiness had been asking to come over for years but one had always managed to find an excuse. Still, we world religious leaders have to show unity these days and so one made an effort. Received him in Scotland of course – they've always been a bit keener on the whole Catholic thing than the English. The DoE seemed to enjoy it, although one had to overrule his plan to greet the Pope dressed as a pregnant nun – not that there is any denying that the look on his face would have been worth it.

Camilla said she thought one was a little harsh to have barred one of His Holiness' little helpers, Cardinal Kasper, for saying Britain was like a Third World country. Explained that religious tolerance does have its limits, even with a loving and gracious Queen at the helm as Supreme Governor. The DoE spent the entire month incessantly calling him 'Kasper the unfriendly Holy Ghost'.

Thought the poor man would never make it, actually: he had a bad flight and said that the food was atrocious. (He wasn't entirely sure what was in the little tinfoil dish but it had apparently played havoc with his constitution. One could relate, having had a very similar experience with Tony Blair.) But we caught up on the 500 years we haven't been speaking and one found time to take him on a quick tour of the Royal Archives to show him how well we've managed without Papal leadership. The DoE gave him a copy of Henry VIII's *Guide to Dealing with the Catholics*, which he thought might be useful. The Pope said he'd read it on the plane home.

It all seemed to go very well, although the text messages haven't stopped since. It started almost as soon as he left and one had sat down to watch *Deal or No Deal*: 'Where did you get your hat/Bentley/palace/husband?' 'Who is Nick Clegg?' etc. One never replied, of course. If there is one thing successive monarchs have learned about pontiffs over the last 500 years, it's not to encourage them.

Come to think of it, not sure what happened vis-à-vis our discussion about the potential beatification of Freddie Mercury. The last thing one heard was the Vatican asking for evidence of miracles performed by him. Sent them Queen's *Miracle* album and a copy of their Live Aid performance on DVD.

Midnight: Got back to Sandringham House. No idea what's happened to Camilla. She 'popped out for a fag' about 11ish and didn't come back.

• THURSDAY 9TH DECEMBER, 2010
'The students are revolting.'

Had hardly had time to finish one's bacon and eggs when reports of unrest in London came in. The students are revolting, as the DoE would say, over tuition fees.

Looks like Mr Clegg is getting the brunt of it. He texted to ask why people did not realise that when he promised to abolish tuition fees before the last election he, like everyone else, never thought for a million years that he'd actually ever be in any position of influence. Would have joined the Conservatives or Labour if he'd have actually wanted to be in power, apparently.

The DoE is having a sympathy protest at Sandringham and burning an effigy of Mr Clegg in the garden. One decided the students had until 8 p.m. to get back to their cold baked beans before one sent down a Royal Water Cannon. Or a Canon of the Church of England if things really got serious. If there is one thing students don't like seeing it's a man of the cloth.

Charles and Camilla are back in London for the Royal Variety Performance and seem to have literally driven into the thick of it. Charles texted to say: 'Hundreds of people turned out to catch a glimpse of Camilla and me. They were excitedly banging on the car.' Typical. One lets one's son borrow the car and it comes back dented and scratched. Apparently some little scoundrel managed to get close enough to poke Camilla with a stick. It's a wonder she didn't get out and tell him what for.

Had a few more troops positioned at Buckingham Palace just in case and went to bed with a gin and tonic.

• FRIDAY 10TH DECEMBER, 2010
'Get down to Parliament Square with a sponge and a bucket of soapy water, Clegg.'

Looks like London had a bit of a battering yesterday. Sent Mr Clegg an early morning text to tell him to be a bit more careful when making promises in the future and, more importantly, to get a bucket of soapy water and a sponge and get down to Parliament Square. Issued a Royal Decree that tuition fees in England shall be raised further to cover the cost of repairs to one's capital city, one's Rolls-Royce and the Duchess of Cornwall.

Charles texted to say: 'Last night's Royal Variety Performance was a riot.' Told him he'd better get one's car fixed pronto. Made a mental note to find the rascal who damaged one's Rolls-Royce, and, when one does, tuition fees will be the least of his worries. Be assured.

- ## SATURDAY 11TH DECEMBER, 2010
'You'd better pay your dues, Ashcroft.'

Up with the cock to look at tax receipts over an Egg McMuffin. Lord Ashcroft is a bit light on the 'paying his dues' front. Sent him a note to tell him he'd better settle up or one would be down on him like a tonne of constitutional bricks, and to remind him that one put the HM into HMRC. Texted Mr Cameron to suggest that in future only those subjects paying tax are considered for elevation to the House of Lords. He replied to assure one that Lord Ashcroft had paid a great deal of money to the Conservative Party instead. Sent the DoE down to London to poke him with a stick.

- ### SUNDAY 12TH DECEMBER, 2010
'Royal X Factor Party at Sandringham.'

Camilla and Charles are back at Sandringham after their 'Royal Variety Riot' in London in time for this evening's Royal *X Factor* Party. They arrived in an armoured tank, just to be on the safe side. If there's one thing Camilla cannot stand it is being poked with a stick. The DoE is back from his day in London and spent the entire evening poking her with a stick and laughing uncontrollably. She said that the car journey had turned out to be endlessly more entertaining than the Royal Variety Performance itself and that Simon Cowell had asked her if she'd appear in a new 'Poke the Duchess' TV series he's planning for next year.

The Royal *X Factor* Party was a huge success. We combined it this year with Queen night and the household staff lined up to sing Queen hits in front of a panel consisting of oneself, the DoE, Prince Andrew and Princess Anne. One's private secretary did a very emotional 'Who Wants to Live Forever', which brought everyone to tears.

11 p.m.: Finished the evening off with a constitutional number of martinis.

• MONDAY 13TH DECEMBER, 2010
'Camilla, is that you in that vase?'

Empire of a hangover. Can't remember a thing about last night but awoke this morning to find Linnet the corgi dyed pink and Camilla upside down in a giant ornamental vase, still smoking. Left her there for a bit, as she seemed quite content, and tucked into a DoE special fry up, consisting of essentially everything it is possible to fry. It's something he learned from one's late mother, HM Queen Elizabeth. She had something of a reputation in Royal circles for breakfasts on an epic scale.

Spent the day hoovering up sequins from last night and trying to wash the pink out of Linnet.

Had Camilla extracted from one's ornamental vase and sloped off for an early night (7 p.m.).

• TUESDAY 14TH DECEMBER, 2010
'Jemima Puddle-Duck (Mr Clegg) on the phone.'

Mr Pickles, the Communities Secretary, sent up a draft of the new localism bill. Wasn't entirely sure what it was all about, to be honest, but made one handwritten amendment to introduce legislation requiring 'Mr Clegg to be known henceforth as Jemima Puddle-Duck', popped it in the red box and sent it back.

Read the police report on the student riots (or 'unrest' as they like to call it). They recommend one seriously consider a water cannon for future unruly behaviour. Seriously considering it for the next State Opening of Parliament.

Popped out in the afternoon for some more wrapping paper. Got stopped in WHSmith by a woman who said one looked just like Helen Mirren.

• **WEDNESDAY 15TH DECEMBER, 2010**
'Anne is reigning in Europe. Nearly partitioned Germany.'

7 p.m.: Had supper on a tray by the TV and watched a documentary about the House of Lords, which turned out to be an episode of *Crimewatch*. The DoE slept throughout the entire thing, awoke just before the end and declared, 'That was good!' before heading up to bed.

• **THURSDAY 16TH DECEMBER, 2010**
'Mr Cameron on the phone. No idea what he's talking about.'

The PM called for a tele audience. He chats away, but all one ever really hears is 'blah, blah, blah, blah'. Still, gives one time to file one's nails. Angled the camera at a painting of one looking attentive and popped out to shoot a pheasant or two for supper. Came back to find the PM still going.

Popped down to the kitchens to deliver the pheasant to find a footman and a kitchen maid in a compromising embrace. He said he was helping her to peel a potato, which one assumed must have been a euphemism. Asked her to pluck the pheasant and told him that wasn't a euphemism.

Christmas presents

1. Anti-shine foundation make-up for Mr Cameron
2. Fisher-Price laptop for Mr Clegg (with animal buttons)
3. 'My First Calculator for' Mr Osborne
4. Nasal decongestant for Mr Miliband
5. Gun for the DoE

6. My Little Pony stable for Edward
7. Idiot's Guide to the Constitution for Charles
8. 500 B&H for Camilla
9. Travel bag for Andrew
10. Hair curlers for Anne
11. Pippa Middleton for Harry
12. Ireland for William

• FRIDAY 17TH DECEMBER, 2010

'46p for a First Class letter? The DoE said he'd take it himself for less than that.'

Posted the last of one's Christmas cards. One can see why one's people are up in arms at the price increases: 46p for a First Class letter? One is seriously considering taking the 'Royal' out of 'Royal Mail'. Although, come to think of it, that would probably mean Mr Clegg or Mr Cameron's head on stamps and one couldn't do that to one's people. Besides which, there's bound to be a law against using the images of small boys for commercial purposes.

Fortnum and Mason delivered a mammoth hamper as a Christmas gift to their sovereign. They send one every year and one likes to let the staff share it out between them. Have decided to get one's Christmas puddings, which all the staff also receive as a present, from Tesco this year though to help with costs. Every little helps.

• SATURDAY 18TH DECEMBER, 2010

'Camilla on the phone. Having a bit of a fire problem with Charles.'

Started the day with a bacon sandwich, a box of Norfolk biscuits and a pot of tea. Camilla called to say that she'd accidentally set fire to the Prince of Wales, but that she'd popped him in a bath of cold water and he seemed to be recovering OK. Was trying to make a crème brûlée, apparently. She said she'd keep a close eye on the situation overnight and that if things weren't looking any better by the morning she could always pop out and buy a crème brûlée instead.

• SUNDAY 19TH DECEMBER, 2010

'Quite frankly, the only place your head will be appearing, Mr Cameron, is on a spike on Tower Bridge. One can assure you.'

Got back from an early morning walk with the corgis and Mr Cameron called about the Royal Mail price increase problem. He said that he would completely understand if one thought it more appropriate for the Prime Minister's head to appear on stamps if one did not want to be associated with such a price. Assured him that one's head will continue to appear on stamps and the only place his head was likely to appear was up on Tower Bridge. He thanked one for being 'very clear, as always, Your Majesty' and said he had to rush off as Mr Clegg was picking at the wallpaper again.

• Monday 20th December, 2010
'Christmas lights are up. There's a bulb blown so the DoE is climbing the tree to locate it.'

Spent the morning in the loft looking for the Christmas decorations and had the family over in the afternoon to decorate the Royal Christmas Tree.

The Norwegians send a tree over every year, which is very generous seeing as one only sends them a box of Stilton and a bottle of port. Went through the usual ritual of putting up all the decorations before switching the lights on and then spending about three hours hunting for the one bulb that had blown, which is particularly difficult when one's tree is approximately twenty five feet high. The DoE finally located the problem and the tree lit up like the Blackpool Illuminations. Caught Andrew round the back eating the chocolate bells, the little rascal.

We all sat round in the evening feeling very Christmassy and eating nuts. No one likes nuts and dried fruit at any other time of the year, but light up a Christmas tree and they can't get enough.

- TUESDAY 21ST DECEMBER, 2010

'Yes, one is letting the Business Secretary stay, although stripped of all power and influence; a state altogether more suited to a Lib Dem.'

Woke to the news that Vince Cable had threatened to quit the Government. Amazing. It had completely passed one by that he was there in the first place. He was soon on the phone, apologising profusely – or something like that. One had actually popped him on hold and gone out for a quick walk with the corgis but he was still chatting away when one got back. Decided to let him stay on as Business Secretary, although stripped of all power and influence; a state altogether more suited to a Liberal Democrat.

Took pity on the Government and decided to distract the media for a while by announcing a second Royal Wedding: one's granddaughter, Zara Phillips. One has agreed that she can marry that Rugby chap on the express condition that he gets his nose sorted beforehand. One can simply not have him marrying into the Royal Family looking like a butcher's window. Nice chap though, and the DoE says he's a 'bloody good Rugby player'. Anne is over the moon. May as well get two Royal Weddings out of the way in one year.

Zara says she'd like to get married in Scotland, which means we'll be able to dust off the official Scottish titles (Prince Charles uses the title the Duke of Rothesay while in Scotland. He also has the titles Earl of Carrick and Baron Renfrew, Lord of the Isles, and Prince and Great Steward of Scotland – although we don't use that one much as it encourages Scottish republicans; Camilla is known as the Duchess of Rothesay, and Princess Tartan; and Prince Andrew has the title Earl of Inverness and Baron Golf. And of course the DoE is still the DoE.)

Spent the afternoon reading the State Papers (otherwise known as the racing papers) and retired with a large gin, happy in the knowledge that politicians of all political hues can be relied upon to be complete and utter idiots and that one's beautiful granddaughter will never again tap one up to pay for Rugby World Cup tickets.

- **WEDNESDAY 22ND DECEMBER, 2010**
'Half a bottle of gin down and feeling positively unconstitutional. Another glass or two and one may have completely forgotten about MPs.'

Up early for a long walk with the corgis. Popped in on one's estate manager for a cup of coffee and a Custard Cream. He said Jeremy Hunt should make the decision on Mr Murdoch's proposed takeover of BSkyB. Sounded like a sensible idea, so one texted Mr Cameron on the way home to suggest it. He's a sensible chap, one's estate manager. Although to be fair his 'Poll Tax' idea in the nineties didn't go down well. Poor old Mrs Thatcher never recovered. Still, as one always says, no idea is a bad idea.

Back in time for lunch and, after half a bottle of gin, found oneself feeling positively unconstitutional. Another glass or two and one may have completely forgotten about MPs. Decided to retire early and watched a few *Open All Hours* DVDs in bed.

- **THURSDAY 23RD DECEMBER, 2010**

'The Pope has recorded a piece for Radio 4. Nice that the Catholics are catching up – in some respects, at least.'

The goose has arrived. The DoE says it's the biggest bird we've had at Sandringham for Christmas since the Duchess of York. Andrew's offered to do the stuffing. The Pope texted to say he's recorded a Christmas piece for Radio 4. One pointed out that the Supreme Governor of the Church of England has been broadcasting at Christmas for decades. Still, nice to know that the Catholics are catching up. One's always been ahead of one's time. The DoE puts it down to a fast watch.

Wrapped the last few presents before dinner. Had to have someone pop out for more wrapping paper for Camilla's. Worried that might have overdone it, but the DoE thinks she'll have them all smoked before Easter. Bought Charles a battery-operated lettuce that talks back.

• FRIDAY 24TH DECEMBER, 2010 –
CHRISTMAS EVE
*'The Middletons have sent a Tesco Value Hamper
up to Sandringham. Awkward.'*

Declared Christmas Eve officially open from the
Royal Bed. Wonders of technology mean it's possible
to reign in sixteen sovereign states without actually
moving a muscle. Of course, as Supreme Governor
of the Church of England, one is somewhat in charge
of Christmas so one likes to take an active interest
and make sure it all goes according to plan.

Mr Clegg called to say he'd bought a packet
of mince pies and a bottle of sherry for Father
Christmas. Camilla called to say she'd left her
stockings on the end of the bed.

Closed the UK at midday so one's people could
do some last minute shopping. Popped down to
the kitchens to check on Christmas lunch
preparations, only to find that the Middletons
had sent over a Tesco Value Hamper. Awkward.

Wonder if it's too late to send them a Christmas card? Probably best not to encourage them: in-laws and stray cats and all that.

The Royal Family started gathering from about 4ish. One's having a political-themed Christmas fancy dress party this evening. The DoE is going as Santa's Little Helper (Mr Clegg), Andrew as Scrooge (Mr Osborne), Charles as the Ghost of Christmas Past (Mr Blair), and Edward as the Christmas Fairy (David Laws).

The Prince of Wales has recorded a Christmas message. He's brought it round on DVD. We'll put it on after lunch tomorrow and pretend it's on TV.

11 p.m.: A couple of Snowballs by the tree and off to bed.

● SATURDAY 25TH DECEMBER, 2010 –
CHRISTMAS DAY
'Listen up, people of the United Kingdom and Commonwealth. One shall address you at

3 p.m. and one's expecting a larger audience than EastEnders.'

Yea, Lord, we greet thee, born this happy morning! Woken up by Edward jumping on one's bed at about 6 a.m. He does get excited at Christmas. We all traipsed downstairs for presents and bacon sandwiches around the tree before heading off to church. The DoE had bought one a cattle prod for use at the State Opening of Parliament. After all these years of marriage he knows just what one wants for Christmas!

Back from church and settled down for one's Christmas message before lunch. One had recorded two Christmas messages this year: one about sport and one declaring a return to absolute monarchy and revoking independence around the world. Only decided to broadcast the sport one this morning; didn't want to spoil Mr Cameron's Christmas by kicking him out on his arse.

One always gets a larger audience than *EastEnders* but it's never publicised. Don't like to let one's people and politicians know the true extent of one's popularity. They might find it threatening. Put Charles' Christmas message on the DVD. We go through this every year and no one ever mentions that it's not actually being broadcast.

Andrew had given the goose a good stuffing and the DoE carved and handed around plates. Usual argument over who does and doesn't like sprouts, and party hats all round. The DoE says a party hat is the closest Charles will get to a crown for a while. Camilla led a game of charades, which the DoE managed to win despite sleeping through about 90 per cent of it, and we all settled down for a night in front of the TV.

- ## Sunday 26th December, 2010
'The DoE has got a fried breakfast on the go.'

Woke up with a colony of midgets hammering nails into one's head. One is never doing

Snakebites again. Ever. The DoE got a light breakfast of bacon, sausages, eggs, beans, potatoes, fried bread, mushrooms, tomatoes and black pudding on the go and we all began to come round. Goodness knows what happened to Camilla. She was singing the National Anthem and swinging from a chandelier when one went to bed. The DoE has gone out with the corgis to see if they can find her.

Charles has broken his talking lettuce already. He's only had it a day. The DoE says he should never have watered it.

Bubble and squeak for supper, a few sweet sherries and an early night.

• MONDAY 27TH DECEMBER, 2010
'Packed a few sandwiches of Christmas dinner leftovers.'

Up and out early for a walk with the corgis. One does love Sandringham at Christmas, although in hindsight one perhaps shouldn't have taken the corgis out in the snow. Poor Monty jumped out of the Land Rover and completely disappeared. It took Camilla about half an hour with a spade before she found the poor thing.

Packed a few sandwiches of assorted Christmas dinner leftovers and wandered over to Wood Farm for a festive picnic lunch. We'll be eating these for weeks. Have sent the PM a slice of Christmas cake in the post. Last year's, that is. Well, it keeps, doesn't it?

Spent the afternoon in front of the fire trying to thaw out Camilla and Monty.

• TUESDAY 28TH DECEMBER, 2010
'Royal game of Twister. Be careful Camilla, you'll put your hip out.'

Decided to have a day in with the family. The DoE made everyone a continental breakfast of toast and jam and an English breakfast of bacon and sausage sandwiches and eggy bread, which got the day off to a good start. Camilla has finally thawed out after retrieving the corgis from the snow yesterday; although one's a bit concerned she may have a touch of frostbite on her hands. She can barely hold a cigar.

Settled down for a game of Twister. Edward is the reigning champion, although all those years of ballet and yoga have put him at a distinct advantage. Camilla managed to get herself stuck in a rather unfortunate position, which was awkward. Thankfully, after several glasses of gin, and with the help of some WD-40, the DoE managed to pop her back into shape.

Spent the evening watching *Charlie and the Chocolate Factory* on TV. The DoE says if he ever finds out that Oompa Loompas actually exist, he's having the entire House of Commons replaced by them. Looking into having existing MPs painted orange in the meantime.

- ## Wednesday 29th December, 2010
'Text from Sir Elton John: "I'm a Queen Mother!"'

Epic lie-in, which extended into the early afternoon.
May well have stayed there all day if one hadn't
been rudely awoken by a text from Sir Elton
John declaring, 'I'm a Queen Mother, I'm a
Queen Mother.' One didn't reply. Apparently he
and David Furnish have adopted a baby. One can
only imagine the sequins that child will have
access to.

- ## Thursday 30th December, 2010
*'Yes, one is indeed a great-grandmother. And, for
that matter, a great Queen.'*

Princess Anne called first thing with the news
that one is indeed a great grandmother. (And,
for that matter, a great Queen.) Immediately
wondered if that was the reason Zara was
getting married, but apparently it's Peter
and Autumn Phillips who have had their first
child. The DoE says he hopes they name her

'Winter' after Autumn. Much excitement in
the Royal Household. There hasn't been a new
baby around since Mr Clegg was appointed
Deputy Prime Minister. Wondered for a minute
if perhaps Peter and Autumn were surrogate
parents for Elton John's new baby but Anne
assures us that the timing is pure coincidence.

- **FRIDAY 31ST DECEMBER, 2010**
*'One wouldn't make you a pantomime dame, Mr
Clegg. Maybe the arse end of a pantomime horse.'*

New Year's Eve. One has published the New
Year's Honours. Seriously considered making Mr
Clegg a Dame (or a Deputy Dame).

Decided to make Annie Lennox a CBE for
services to Scottish independence, prompting
a text from the Pope: 'Why?' Very funny. Also
published the New Year's Dishonours, which
this year went to the entire Cabinet and Richard
Madeley. Decided in the end not to knight Mr
Cameron, although there is a strong possibility

that he'll find his monarch visiting him with a
sword before the year is out.

New Year's Resolutions:
1. Cause one's politicians as much misery as is
   Royally possible
2. Keep American independence under constant
   and very close review. Any sodding around
   and Obama is out on his arse
3. Order gin in bulk to save costs
4. Pop over to Ireland to collect the debt
5. Sort Bono problem
6. Sell France

In the United Kingdom and throughout the
world, 2011 is celebrated as the 'Year of the
Queen'. This is the fifty ninth consecutive such
year.

Had a small New Year Party at Sandringham
for about five hundred close friends and family.
All gathered around at midnight to pull party
poppers. Apart from Andrew. He'd arrived in full

military uniform and thought it more appropriate to go outside and fire a cannon. A couple of verses of 'Auld Lang Syne', which no one actually knows the words to but loves to hum, and dancing until the small hours.

- SATURDAY 1ST JANUARY, 2011
'I declare 2011 officially open. May God bless you. I wish you, and all those whom you love and care for, a very happy New Year. Elizabeth R.'

Queen Mother of all hangovers. Minor problem at Sandringham. Awoke to news that the DoE is stuck atop a statue, where he's been since 3 a.m. apparently. Camilla noticed him, having popped out for an early morning walk. William came over with a helicopter and a bit of rope and we had him down by midday. No idea how he got up there but he said there was a wonderful view.

Mr Cameron called to wish one a Happy New Year. He was on the phone for about half an hour but all one heard was 'blah blah blah blah blah'.

Had the family over for New Year's Day lunch, although we were all somewhat subdued. Polished off the last of the Christmas Stilton in front of a special New Year edition of *Who Wants to be a Millionaire?* The DoE has applied every year but has never been selected to appear.

Spent the evening flicking through one's diary for the year ahead: State Visit to Ireland, State Visit by the Obamas, two Royal Weddings . . . it's going to be a busy one.

Shopping list

1. Case of gin
2. Ireland
3. BBQ Pringles
4. Nutcracker for audiences with the PM
5. Birthday present for Mr Clegg (special edition My Little Pony?)

6. Coco Pops
7. Crate of tonic
8. Dubonnet
9. That nice bit of Spain

The Arab Spring, Valentine's Day and the Brit Awards

- Tuesday 1st February, 2011

'Text from George Osborne: "Pinch, punch, first of the month and no returns." Moron.'

February already. One doesn't know where the year is going. Back to London this week. One shall be sad to leave Sandringham behind. Mr Osborne sent his customary 'pinch, punch, first of the month and no returns' text. Really must speak to that lad, especially as one seems to have slipped into the higher rate of tax bracket.

Looks like it's all kicking off in Egypt. President Mubarak texted to ask if one 'had a spare room'. The DoE thinks by the end of the week he'll be 'walking like an Egyptian'. King Abdullah seems to have pre-empted any trouble his end. He texted to say he was 'having a bit of a sort out' with his cabinet. Thankfully, the only time one has crowds outside the Palace in London they're waving flags and singing 'God Save the Queen'.

Mr Cameron sent a link to the new 'crime maps' that he's releasing. A couple of clicks and one can see the level of crime in any particular area. Had a cursory glance but there seems to be a glitch in the system, as it's not showing the massive amount of crime committed at Downing Street. Text the PM to point it out. No reply.

4 p.m.: As it's a Tuesday, ended the day with a large G&T with almost no ice.

- WEDNESDAY 2ND FEBRUARY, 2011
'One is Pharaoh of Egypt, but keeping a low profile.'

Up early for a quick review of State Papers.

Sir Gus called to ask if one was aware that Mr Clegg knocks off at 3 p.m. every day. Not having that. He's getting a full-time salary. Got him on the phone and explained that he is required to work beyond his milk break and nap at 3 p.m. and if that means missing children's TV then so be it. He said there were good reasons why he couldn't work a full day but sadly one had hung up before he had a chance to go through them. If there was one good thing about Mrs Thatcher, it was that she wasn't scared of a bit of hard work.

The Egypt revolution shows no sign of abating. Not looking good for Mubarak. One is, of course, technically still Pharaoh of Egypt, but keeping a low profile. The DoE called the British Museum to ask which Egyptian artefacts they were missing, just in case the opportunity arose to complete the collection.

3 p.m.: Knocked off for an exceptionally early gin.

• THURSDAY 3RD FEBRUARY, 2011
'Mrs Cameron and Princess Anne are discussing hairstyles. Hopefully Mrs Cameron will pick up some tips.'

The Camerons are here for their annual Sandringham visit. They arrived last night but one couldn't face them. Not with the current crisis in Egypt to deal with. Had almost escaped out with the corgis when one bumped into them in the hallway, grinning like idiots. Really, that man is the only man one knows whose Madame Tussauds waxwork looks more lifelike than he does. Mrs Cameron's always very pleasant, though. At least she can manage a curtsey, which is more than Mrs Blair ever did. One always smiled when she made such a big thing in public about not bowing down to anyone, when in private she insisted that the lack of a curtsey was down to bad knees and that she was petrified that she may for ever be locked in a half-kneeling position.

Left Mrs Cameron with Princess Anne to pick up a few fashion tips and took Mr Cameron out for a walk with the corgis. Handy actually to have someone else in charge of the poo bag. He said that, all things considered, his first year in office had gone rather well. One told him that, all things considered, he was lucky to still be in office and that if he didn't show some immediate improvement Mr Mubarak wouldn't be the only one walking like an Egyptian. He said he was grateful for the feedback.

Willow the corgi seems to have taken a distinct dislike to Mr Cameron and has started biting him on the arse every time the poor chap bends down. He laughs it off but one worries he's feeling a little bullied. Quite convinced that Monty is in on it: he has a poo, Mr Cameron bends down to pick it up and Willow sinks her teeth into his posterior.

Got back mid-afternoon to find the DoE on the phone to MI6, issuing a few orders about Egypt. At least he thought he was. One has had the number diverted to the talking clock. He hasn't noticed.

Rather awkward dinner with Mr and Mrs Cameron. One does wish she wouldn't do that at the table. Lightened the mood afterwards with a few bottles of vintage port and an epic cheeseboard and Mr Cameron finally seemed to be enjoying himself. That is until he bent over to pop another log on the fire and Willow the corgi took the opportunity to sink her jaws into his nether regions. Brought a tear to the DoE's eye. They disappeared upstairs with a bottle of TCP, and the DoE and I finished off the port and cheese before retiring.

- FRIDAY 4TH FEBRUARY, 2011
'Dear Members of the Cabinet, if you don't start making progress, none of you will be receiving your Duke of Edinburgh's Gold Award.'

Thank Crunchie it's Friday.

The Camerons were already at breakfast when one came down. Mr Cameron looked slightly awkward trying to eat a bowl of Coco Pops standing up, but apparently Willow had rendered him incapable of sitting. Sent out for another bottle of TCP for him to take back to

London. One didn't like to make him feel worse but broke the news that the Cabinet would not be receiving their Duke of Edinburgh's Gold Award unless they started making some serious progress.

Found a spare cushion for the PM's car and waved them off mid-afternoon. The DoE spent the rest of the day chuckling to himself before finally confessing that he'd replaced the TCP he gave to the PM with vinegar.

Ended the day approximately 7/8 full of gin.

• SATURDAY 5TH FEBRUARY, 2011
'The next time Mr Cameron comes round, one is turning one's light off.'

Quiet day at Sandringham. Knitted Edward a cardigan. Back on the gin in the evening and watched *Take Me Out*. The next time Mr Cameron comes round, one is turning one's light off. No likey no lighty.

- ### SUNDAY 6TH FEBRUARY, 2011
'God Save the King.'

Fifty nine years in charge today. Fifty nine years since one's father, King George VI, passed away in this very house. It's the bitter irony of monarchy: losing a father and gaining a world. One wonders if one was too young to reign. Papa was certainly too young to die. And Mummy never truly got over it. Had a sweet sherry and sat quietly by the fire.

- ### MONDAY 7TH FEBRUARY, 2011
'One's Australian PM, Ms Gillard, on the phone; it's embarrassing.'

Heading back to London this afternoon. Started the day with a phone call from one's Australian PM, Ms Gillard. No idea what she said. She can barely talk; it's embarrassing. Sent a message to the Governor-General and asked him to assure one's Australian people that their Queen loves them and to hang on in there.

Mr Cameron sent a message to say that
the ASBO replacement, the new 'Criminal
Behaviour Order', comes into effect today.
Issued the first one on Mr Cameron.

OK people. Your undoubted and gracious Queen
and Sovereign Lady is on Her way back to London
and She's ready to rock. Here comes the reign.

• TUESDAY 8TH FEBRUARY, 2011
*'Mr Schofield, what are you doing for the next five
years?'*

Back in London. Determined to get straight
back to work with a vengeance but got slightly
waylaid watching *This Morning*. Seriously
considering asking Phillip Schofield to form
a Government (it would delight the Queen
of Spain if he did – she's asked him to form a
Spanish Government several times).

Called one's private secretary in and jotted down
a few ideas for a showbiz cabinet:

- Phillip Schofield, PM
- Holly Willoughby, Deputy PM
- Chris Evans, Home Secretary
- Stephen Fry, Minister for Culture, Media and Sport
- Brian May, Minister for Music, Space and Foxes
- Jeremy Clarkson, Minister for Transport and Foreign Secretary
- That nice policeman from *Crimewatch*, Justice Secretary
- Johnny Ball, Chancellor

Prince Edward burst in dressed head to toe in sequins and exclaimed, 'Did somebody say showbiz?', which rather took the edge off of the idea.

- WEDNESDAY 9TH FEBRUARY, 2011
'Wednesday is cancelled, due to lack of interest.'

Life shall resume on Thursday.

- ### Thursday 10th February, 2011

'Text from the Pope: "Is Your Majesty still Pharaoh of Egypt?" Well, yes.'

News from Europe: apparently one is breaking the law by not allowing those staying at one's pleasure to vote. Strange; one thought one made the bloody law. Texted the President of the European Union (like everyone else in the United Kingdom, one doesn't know his name) and pointed out that the irony of criminals voting for criminals was not lost on the Queen. And told him to sod off and concentrate on meddling on the Continent, where it was needed and seemingly welcome.

It's all gone a bit pyramids-up for Mubarak. He texted first thing to say, 'And now, the end is here, and so I face the final curtain,' but had a last minute change of heart and decided to address the nation. It's probably fair to say that his speech was not as well received as one's Christmas broadcasts, and by the end of the day he was contemplating resignation again. ('Should I stay or should I go now? If I go there will be trouble. If I stay there will be double.')

Considering having a couple of pyramids shipped over while no one is looking; they'd look lovely in the British Museum and the DoE says it would mean that there is officially more of Egypt in London than there is in Egypt.

The Pope texted to ask if one was still Pharaoh of Egypt. Well, yes.

- **FRIDAY 11TH FEBRUARY, 2011**
'Who can take a rainbow, wrap it in a sigh? Soak it in the sun and make a groovy lemon pie? The Sovereign . . . Oh the Sovereign can . . .'

Text from Mubarak: 'I think the speech did the trick: thousands of people on the streets celebrating that I'm staying.' That's it. One's not waiting any longer. One can confirm that one has dissolved President Mubarak.

Pile of expenses cheques to sign in the afternoon.
One's personal assistant has to bribe one to do it
by buying enormous bags of Maltesers. Crossed
out a few claims (Mr Cameron: sunbed costs,
perfume for Angela Merkel; Mr Clegg: crayons,
In the Night Garden sweater, jigsaw puzzle; Mr
Osborne: My First Calculator, Ireland).

After a busy day Queening and Pharaohing, one
settled down for a well deserved gin.

• SATURDAY 12TH FEBRUARY, 2011
'Someone get one a fried egg sandwich.'

One seems to have accidently mummified
oneself in gin last night. One puts it down to
Middle East-induced stress. Was just tucking
into a fried egg sandwich when Mubarak phoned,
wondering if there was any chance he could take
over in Ireland. Awkward. Although perhaps not
such a bad idea. Told him one would get back to
him if the Bono situation worsened.

Early Gin O'Clock to combat the hangover.

- ### SUNDAY 13TH FEBRUARY, 2011
'Mr Clegg, why don't you try working beyond 3 p.m.?'

Pissing with rain. Took the corgis out for a wander around Windsor Great Park and came back looking like one had been dragged out of the lake. Camilla said it was the longest walk she'd ever had, but one suspects that it just felt like that as it was too wet to light a fag.

Mr Clegg called about midday. Bit upset; worried that he's not doing a good enough job. One suggested he might try working beyond 3 p.m.

Royal Dancing on Ice Fancy Dress Party at the Castle this evening. All very exciting. The DoE is coming as Jason, Charles is coming as Phillip Schofield, Camilla is a very convincing Emma Bunton and Edward is Karen.

Turned over just in time to see the BAFTA winners. Nice to see that *The King's Speech* did so well, although no one thought to thank His Majesty King George VI. Still, as long as the costume people got due credit, that's the main thing, surely. Sent a message of congratulations to Colin Firth and Helena Bonham Carter, along with an invoice for due royalties arising from use of Royal names, styles and titles, amounting to approximately 75 per cent of the gross, which one thought was exceptionally generous.

The DoE gave a 'King's Speech' to the staff about the desperate lack of gin in the Palace. They apparently thought a case would have lasted the weekend.

• TUESDAY 15TH FEBRUARY, 2011
'Having a lion brought into Downing Street.'

Awoke to news that Mr Cameron has purchased a cat to chase the rats out of Downing Street. The DoE thought that Mr Cameron would have learned his lesson about letting abandoned strays in after the whole Mr Clegg episode. Still, let's hope the cat does the trick. Seriously considering sending in a lion if the rat problems persist (for 'rats' read 'politicians').

Had hardly enough time to finish a bacon and egg sandwich before Mr Clegg called. Very upset and worried the Downing Street cat will replace him in Mr Cameron's affections. Says he tried to catch the rats but they were just too fast for him.

Linnet the corgi actually farts every single time the Prime Minister is on the TV.

Settled down for an evening in front of the TV to watch the Brit Awards. Not sure Kylie is nominated for anything this year but Edward wore his 'Spinning Around' gold hotpants just in case. He loves Kylie.

Caught a glimpse of Justin Bieber; lovely little girl and such a sweet voice. Mildly dismayed at the sight of Boris Becker presenting an award though. Who the hell let him in? Sent a stern text to Border Control to ask what was going on.

The DoE said that if Cheryl Cole won a Brit Award he'd have MI5 clear the place. Luckily she didn't. And who let Boy George out of prison? Pencilled in Cee Lo Green for the Royal Wedding. Tiny Tim's off the list after that dreadful performance, though. It's nights like this that one really misses Freddie Mercury. Had an emotional conversation with Brian May after a few sherries and agreed that he'd play the National Anthem from one's roof again for the Diamond Jubilee.

• **WEDNESDAY 16TH FEBRUARY, 2011**
'Calm down boys, this isn't X Factor.'

Eric Pickles, the rather large Communities Secretary, called first thing to run one through his plan to have local councils vote on executive pay. The DoE and I had a quick vote on Eric Pickles' salary. It's not looking good for the big man. The DoE is convinced that Mr Pickles is a character from *Thomas the Tank Engine*, but we can't say it out loud as Edward gets overexcited.

Decided to send William and Catherine to Canada in July for their first official trip and to check out some holiday-palace options. One's rather fond of Canada. Still seriously considering having it moved closer. Might swap it with Ireland.

There's been much excitement in the Royal Household about the new series of *Masterchef*. Andrew has had his chopper out all day. Settled down to the show but were all disappointed that they'd adopted some *X Factor*-style format of auditions. It never ceases to amaze the Queen how prepared one's people are to embarrass themselves on TV.

• THURSDAY 17TH FEBRUARY, 2011
'You'll be going before the forests, Mr Cameron, one can assure you.'

Up early to instruct Mr Cameron not to sell
one's forests. He texted back to say, 'Sorry Your
Majesty, couldn't see the wood for the trees.
Have dropped the "stupid policy" as instructed.'
Looking into an alternative plan to sell off Vince
Cable to logging companies.

Camilla called before lunch. Absolutely distraught
to discover *The Archers* is fictional. She'd thought
Ambridge was a lovely little village when she
visited, although was rather surprised by the
huge radio studio and wondered why no one ever
mentioned it. Only discovered the truth when
she saw herself in the morning papers. One
assured her that there are many things in life that
seem real but which are in reality an elaborate
hoax – like democracy, for example.

Thought it was about time one had the Obamas
over for an official appraisal. They're coming in
May. Have made it clear that if he turns up with a
bloody American TV box set as a present again one
is having him put straight back on the plane with

his Revocation of Independence papers and DVDs stuffed somewhere that Air Force One doesn't fly.

That man needs almost constant management. Still, he's marginally better than George W Bush, who for his entire term didn't have the foggiest idea that he was president. Which was ironic really, as the rest of the world spent his entire term wishing he wasn't.

● FRIDAY 18TH FEBRUARY, 2011
'OK people. Enough is enough. Home time.'

Spent the morning ruling the Federation of Saint Kitts and Nevis. It's a federal two-island nation in the West Indies, in the Leeward Islands, and the smallest sovereign state in the Americas, so monarchical duties are fairly straightforward. Much like ruling the Isle of Wight, actually, but better weather. It's been in the family since Queen Anne kicked the Spanish out in 1713.

Now, there's a Queen who knew how to rule efficiently. She apparently got tired of ruling in England and Scotland and in 1707 had them lumped together as Great Britain. Continued to reign separately in Ireland though, due to the extra special attention required. She was the first monarch to appoint her husband as Lord High Admiral, which isn't a bad birthday present idea for the DoE. One's made a note.

6 p.m.: Enjoyed Saint Kitts and Nevis so much that one stayed on until the afternoon and finished off the day with a gin and tonic with a paper umbrella.

- SATURDAY 19TH FEBRUARY, 2011
'Get your hand in your pocket, Barclays Bank; you owe one some tax.'

Started the morning by flicking through one's tax receipts. Despite making enormous profits, Barclays Bank seem to have forgotten to pay one any tax. Something about losses the year before or something. Sent them a memo instructing them to get their hands in their pockets and pay up. Thieving bastards, as the DoE would say.

Gordon Brown called after lunch. Something about being misunderstood. Couldn't really understand what he was saying. Popped him on hold and took the corgis out for a spin in the Range Rover. He was still chatting away when one returned about 5ish. Told him it was all very interesting and one would see what one could do but if he didn't mind one was a little tied up ruling sixteen sovereign nations, supremely governing a Church and defending a faith and so really had to crack on.

6 p.m.: Amazed to see the Duchess of York on the evening news complaining about not being invited to the Royal Wedding. She was invited. Unfortunately she sold her invitation to Mr Clegg.

11 p.m.: Embalmed in gin as a tribute to the Egyptian revolution.

- ## Sunday 20th February, 2011
'Considering having the clocks brought forward an hour for reasons of a gin-related nature.'

More comment in the Sunday papers about the guest list for the Royal Wedding. David Beckham's been invited because of William's football connections. Hopefully someone will read the invitation to him. One does hope he doesn't bring Victoria with him. The DoE thinks she always has a face 'like a corgi licking piss off a stinging nettle'. One can see where he's coming from.

Considering having the clocks brought forward an hour for reasons of a gin-related nature. Have told Mr Cameron to look into it. He'll probably wrap it up as 'economic reasons', which is a politician's standard excuse for doing anything.

Settled down for *Dancing on Ice* and made a mental note that the Madeleys are getting a family ASBO, or whatever it's called now. Really, one wonders if any of this year's contestants can legitimately be called celebrities. Chloe Madeley was introduced as a 'TV presenter'. As far as one is aware, the only thing she has ever presented is her driving licence to the police. Text ITV to make enquiries.

- MONDAY 21ST FEBRUARY, 2011
'OK Gaddafi, saddle up the camel.'

It's all gone a bit strange in Libya. Colonel Gaddafi texted to say he'd had a particularly 'shit day'. Told him to saddle up the camel: his days are numbered by the look of it. Sent Mr Cameron over to Egypt to show him what happens if he sods around.

Had settled down to some 'removal of Arab dictators' work when Mr Clegg called. Very upset that his entry in the Blue Peter Diamond Jubilee Emblem Competition wasn't chosen. Bit tearful. One assured him that one is sending him a Blue Peter Badge all the same and he seemed to cheer up a bit. He's been very sensitive since that cat moved in to Downing Street.

• TUESDAY 22ND FEBRUARY, 2011

'No, Mr Clegg, "Gaddafi" is not a Welsh flower.'

Decided, with the trouble in the Middle East, that one is not attending London Fashion Week. This despite being a Fashion Queen and something of an icon for women worldwide.

Mr Cameron's still out in Egypt. Getting a bit carried away by the look of it. Text to tell him that the jolly was over and it was time to get back on the plane. He's the last thing the Middle East needs at the moment. And the DoE is worried he'll melt in the heat.

3 p.m.: News of the Libya situation has finally reached Mr Clegg, who until now had thought 'Gaddafi' was a Welsh flower. Awkward. Camilla came over in the afternoon with a few ideas about how best to respond to the Arab Spring, which she thought was a hotel near Staines.

• **Wednesday 23rd February, 2011**
*'Cameron has sent "apologies" for this afternoon's
audience with his Queen. One has sent "apologies"
for not paying him as a result.'*

Wednesday is usually 'make the Prime Minister
uncomfortable day' but Mr Cameron has sent
'apologies' for missing this afternoon's audience on
account of still being in the Middle East. One sent
back 'apologies' for not paying him as a result. It's a
shame really, as the DoE was going to walk past the
window dressed as Colonel Gaddafi. Thought the look
on Mr Cameron's face would have been priceless.

Mr Hague called during *Midsomer Murders* to discuss
evacuation of one's people from Libya, where it's all
looking a bit horrid. Told him to stop talking and get
one's people on a plane before one gets him out of
Government. That man is an international
embarrassment. And he ruined the end of *Midsomer
Murders*. Text Sir Gus to ask him to get round to the
Foreign Office and pull someone's hair.

7 p.m.: Decided to tackle the Libya situation with an uncharacteristically large gin and tonic.

• THURSDAY 24TH FEBRUARY, 2011
'Colonel Gaddafi, you are not "like the Queen of England". The Queen is still in control of her realms, for a start. And much better looking.'

Well, the Government seem to have completely cocked up the evacuation of British subjects from Libya. One would think that sending over a boat and a couple of planes would be reasonably straightforward for a global superpower, but apparently not. Told Mr Cameron to get on the TV and apologise for the fiasco before one had him evacuated from Downing Street.

Amazing TV broadcast from Colonel Gaddafi, likening himself to me. Was just dialling his number to put him straight on a few things when he texted to say, 'Oh, oobee doo, I wanna be like you. I wanna walk like you, talk like you, reign like you.' Loser. Replied to assure him that he was not 'like the

Queen of England'. The Queen is still in control of her realms, for a start. And much better looking.

He seems to have had quite an impact on Andrew though, who's pitched a tent in the garden and surrounded himself with female bodyguards. The DoE says all he needs is a camel.

- **Friday 25th February, 2011**
'Having some (all?) bishops transferred to Rome, where the standards are lower.'

Headed back to Windsor for a special lunch with the Archbishop of Canterbury and a gaggle of senior bishops. One does like having them over but they all insist on saying grace before eating and if there's one thing a Queen cannot stand it's cold fish fingers. Had a long conversation about conversions to the Catholic Church. After much persuading, one agreed that they didn't all have to go.

The Archbishop said he was considering increasing the amount charged for marrying in a Church of

England church. One said that was fine but to wait until after William and Zara's weddings as one was having enough trouble making ends meet as it was.

- **SATURDAY 26TH FEBRUARY, 2011**
'Absolutely sod all on TV.'

Spent a full day weeding the Windsor Castle Round Tower garden with Camilla. She said she wasn't entirely sure what was a weed and what wasn't so pulled up everything just in case. The DoE spent the day creosoting the fence before nearly taking the arse out of Willow the corgi with a strimmer.

8 p.m.: Night in front of the TV. Having ITV taken off the air.

- **SUNDAY 27TH FEBRUARY, 2011**
'Text from Nick Clegg: "Have cut short my holiday to deal with the Gandhi situation." '

Up early and out for a ride around Windsor Great Park with one's private secretary. One sometimes wishes that politicians could display the strength, grace, loyalty and intelligence of a horse. The DoE says the only similarity is the long faces and the tendency to 'shit on things you really wish they hadn't'.

11 a.m.: Got back to a text from Mr Clegg saying he'd cut short his holiday to 'deal with the Gandhi situation'. One assumes he means 'Gaddafi'. Still, partitioning of Libya may be an option. If there's one thing we Brits like to do it's partition a country.

• MONDAY 28TH FEBRUARY, 2011
'Text from Colonel Gaddafi: "Any chance of laying low at your place for a while?"'

Back to London for the new working week. Reigning 9 to 5, what a way to make a living. The

M4 is a nightmare on a Monday morning so one took the helicopter. Circled over Downing Street for a while to make Mr Cameron nervous and seriously considered razing the place to the ground.

The Libya situation looks like it'll get worse before it gets better. President Sarkozy called to say he'd sent two planes to assist with the evacuation. Good of him to make the entire French Air Force available.

Prime Minister Berlusconi called to say he was a bit embarrassed that Libya had sent a plane to evacuate young women from Italy. Awkward. And Colonel Gaddafi texted to ask, 'Any chance of laying low at your place for a while? I have a tent.' Perhaps he can move in with Andrew. And it's not a 'place'; it is a 'palace'.

Agenda:
Phone call with the Pope

1. Catholic performance over the past 500 years
2. Beatification of Freddie Mercury
3. Possible conversion to Catholicism of all former British prime ministers
4. Improvements in British weather

5. Defending the Faith
6. Bullying of the Archbishop of Canterbury — one won't stand for it

MARCH

Spring Cleaning and Lent

- **Friday 4th March, 2011**

'Hoping the gin deficit is less serious than analysts predict.'

Rang for one's usual Thursday morning constitutional, only to be told that the household has inexplicably run out of gin, and that 'someone is popping over to Harvey Nics to get some more'.

Heads will roll.

- **Wednesday 9th March, 2011**

'There are times when one must make sacrifices. And then there's Gin O'Clock.'

As Supreme Governor of the Church of England, one decided to set a good example to one's flock and give up something for Lent. The DoE suggested giving up Australia, since it's so far away, but one couldn't do that to Rolf Harris.

- Friday 18th March, 2011
'Having a bit of toast. Then might send the RAF into Libya.'

International ructions force one to break one's diary fast. Have texted the Archbishop of Canterbury to keep him in the Lent loop.

Ran out of patience and decided to send the RAF into Libya. Had a slice of toast first. One never goes to war on an empty stomach. Mr Cameron is very excited. Not sure what it is about being prime minister, but they always seem to want to be remembered for some kind of military conflict.

Title ideas for one's published diary extracts

1. Reigning in One's Heart
2. Reigning Men
3. Killer Queen
4. Gin O'Clock
5. Me, My Crown and I
6. Diary of a Beauty Queen

7. Dancing Queen
8. One and One
9. Life with a Duke of Hazard
10. Queen's Greatest Hits
11. Here Comes the Reign Again

April Fools' Day, Easter, One's Birthday and the Royal Wedding

'Come out of the Downing Street loo, Mr Clegg; one was only kidding.'

April Fools' Day: Sent a memo to all Commonwealth prime ministers and to presidents of the former British dominions (which is most of the world):

Dear presidents and prime ministers,

For the last fifty nine years, one has watched with interest your attempts to self-govern. It is now clear to the Queen that this experiment in democracy has failed. I hereby revoke all independence, dissolve parliaments throughout the Commonwealth and former dominions and declare an immediate return to direct rule and absolute monarchy. For the avoidance of doubt, this will require proper English spelling and pronunciation to be restored in America forthwith.

With immediate effect, responsibility will be delegated to Princess Anne (equestrian matters),

Prince Charles (matters of the environment, religion and architecture), the DoE (press regulation, corporal punishment, foreign affairs and tax collection), Prince Andrew (international trade and golf), Prince Harry (defence), Prince William (sport and marriage guidance), the Duchess of Cornwall (alcohol and tobacco) and Prince Edward (the arts). Any problems, don't hesitate to call.

Your ever-loving and gracious Queen, Pharaoh, Empress, Paramount Chief, Supreme Governor, Duke, Lord and Defender of the Faith,

EIIR

Most took it in the spirit it was intended, although Mr Clegg apparently locked himself in the Downing Street loo for about five hours. Mr Obama called to ask if it would be possible to take it seriously as he is really not enjoying this whole president thing. One said one would give it some serious thought and get back to him with an answer when he comes over for his annual appraisal in May.

Mr Osborne sent over the national balance sheet, which sadly was not an April Fool joke.

• MONDAY 18TH APRIL, 2011
'Watching Meet the Middletons on C4. Awkward.'

It's birthday week. One has had Easter timed to coincide this year as an excuse for a long weekend. Informed one's people that their gracious and loving Queen had provided them with a four day week and got started on final Royal Wedding plans. The DoE revealed his wedding outfit, which he'd selected purely to see the look on Mr Middleton's face. After much discussion, one felt compelled to insist that he stick with the traditional morning dress instead.

Considered a last minute addition of Brian May playing the 'Wedding March' from the roof of Westminster Abbey. Asked one's private secretary to get on the phone to see if he's available at short notice. One can't imagine he has a lot on these days. The Archbishop of Canterbury called to say that there were religious reasons that made rock music in a church 'difficult'. Told him that there are Supreme Governor and Defender of the Faith reasons why one could make his life 'difficult'. He seemed happy with that as a compromise.

Mrs Middleton texted to say she could do one a 'great family deal on mail order bunting for the Buck Pal balcony' but only if one ordered online before 5 p.m. and excluding postage and packing. No thank you.

9 p.m.: Dinner and few gin and tonics and settled down with the DoE to watch Channel 4's documentary on the Middletons. Thoroughly awkward. One does hope they all manage to be better dressed for the wedding. The DoE thinks six places at the wedding for the Middleton family is approximately five places too many. Must review the seating plan.

• TUESDAY 19TH APRIL, 2011

'Yes, one's largest RAF aircraft in history –
Voyager – has arrived in the UK. This will
principally be used for the movement of gin.'

Mr Brown on the phone first thing. Wanting
to know if one would appoint him as the next
Managing Director of the International Monetary
Fund (IMF). One explained that one doesn't
like speaking to prime ministers while they are
actually prime ministers, certainly doesn't like
speaking to them once one's people have come
to their senses and voted them out of office and
that one absolutely and unequivocally would not
be appointing him managing director of a local
dog track, let alone of the IMF. He seemed to
take that well.

Had barely time to consume a constitutional
bacon and egg sandwich when Mr Clegg jumped
on the IMF bandwagon asking, 'What's the IMF?
Do I get the casting vote on Gordon Brown? Do
I, do I, do I?!' One didn't reply. Text-enabling

Fisher-Price mobiles was the worst thing they ever did; one never gets a minute of peace now Mr Clegg can communicate.

Spent the day at the Palace keeping the United Kingdom on track and at the forefront of global thinking. Very excited to finally take delivery of one's largest RAF aircraft, the *Voyager*. This is the largest RAF plane in history and will principally be used for the movement of gin around the Commonwealth and intimidation of the French.

9 p.m.: Dinner, gin, Dubonnet, slice of lemon under the ice and bed.

- WEDNESDAY 20TH APRIL, 2011
'Now Charles, that's not very democratic.'

Charles and Camilla came over at the crack of dawn to celebrate Prince Charles becoming the longest-serving heir apparent in British history. As a special treat, one let him rule Australia today and Camilla was there to watch. Had to point out that summary dismissal of a prime minister is frowned upon these days, although in the case of Ms Gillard there would probably be widespread agreement.

It's always an awkward time, talking about Charles' wait for the throne as heir apparent. Lucky the mood was lightened by a text from Nick Clegg saying he 'didn't think Prince Charles' hair was that long'. Heaven help us.

Decided, as it's one's birthday tomorrow, to have an early gin and tonic. Got slightly carried away and nearly forgot that Charles was still ruling Australia. Could have been very difficult. Who knows what he might have done overnight. Camilla said she'd had a most enjoyable day and that the weather had been lovely.

• THURSDAY 21st APRIL, 2011
'Happy Birthday to me, Happy Birthday to me, Happy Birthday my Majesty, Happy Birthday to me!'

Birthday! Whoop whoop! One does love birthdays. It's such a shame they only come twice a year. The DoE brought one a bacon sandwich and a bowl of Coco Pops in bed on a little tray with a flower on it and Edward sat on the end of the bed opening one's cards. Nothing from Mr Clegg. Sent him a text to point out that he appears to have forgotten to send his undoubted Queen and Sovereign Lady a birthday card and suggesting he get one sent round this minute. He replied to say he was just finishing the colouring in.

The Pope texted to say 'Hey Birthday Girl. How YOU doing?!' One's not replying.

Popped over to the Maundy Thursday service at Westminster Abbey. In an act of lovingness and grace, we Queens like to give out some pennies to pensioners on our birthday. Took the Bentley via Downing Street on the way home to remind Mr Cameron who's in charge and to drop off a bag of excess pennies to Mr Osborne to help with the deficit reduction.

Arrived back at the Palace to a Happy Birthday email from the Chancellor. Texted him to remind him that an email does not constitute a birthday card and suggested he get his crayons out and get drawing before one sent round his P45.

Ireland-themed fancy dress party in the evening. William and Harry came as Jedward, Andrew as Bob Geldof, Edward as Louis Walsh and Charles as a leprechaun. Camilla misread the invitation as 'Iceland-themed fancy dress' and came as a volcano. Had a quite unconstitutional amount of gin for reasons of a birthday and Bank Holiday nature and fell asleep on the sofa.

- **Friday 22nd April, 2011 – Good Friday**
'One's wedding hat has arrived.'

The morning after the night before. Thank goodness it's a Bank Holiday. Woken about 11 a.m. by a text from the Pope saying 'have a Good Friday'. Funny.

God knows what happened to Camilla. Her volcano outfit is out on the terrace, still smoking, but there's no sign of her. Perhaps she wandered back to Clarence House.

Authorised Easter, and with the day's Supreme Governor of the Church of England duties over for Good Friday, settled down to a hot cross bun and a sweet sherry.

4 p.m.: One's Royal Wedding hat has arrived. Keeping the colour a secret though in case Camilla puts a bet on it. Tried it on and the DoE said one looked very fetching. Was considering wearing the Imperial State Crown but one never likes to overshadow the bride at a wedding. Still, one will of course arrive to a full fanfare by the state trumpeters. There are standards to maintain, after all.

- SATURDAY 23RD APRIL, 2011
'Mrs Middleton on the phone. Wanting to check "our outfits don't clash on the big day".'

Had some quiet time this morning so decided to review the Royal Wedding seating plan. The

Beckhams?! Jesus, one had forgotten they were coming. Can they even speak?! William said he had felt compelled to ask since taking over as President of the Football Association. And Victoria Beckham too. The DoE says she looks like she's constantly chewing a bad scallop. Really, this is a Royal Wedding, not *Friday Night with Jonathan Ross*. Oh God, Jonathan Ross isn't coming is he? No. Thank Christ for small mercies.

Had Mrs 'call me Carole' Middleton on the phone after lunch. Wanting to check 'our outfits don't clash on the big day'. One seriously doubts they would. And one does wish she wouldn't insist on calling one 'Liz'. She said she had done a deal for a job lot of party bags and was one interested? Could apparently have a crown printed on them for another £1.28 per unit.

Seating plan revised. Victoria Beckham shall be seated so far back she'll practically be in Surrey. Popped her behind a pillar too. Don't want to cause unnecessary alarm to the other guests.

10 p.m.: Finished the day approximately ¾ full of Pimm's, ¼ full of strawberries and cream.

• SUNDAY 24TH APRIL, 2011 – EASTER SUNDAY
'I wish you all, and those whom you love and care for, a very happy Easter.'

Church this morning for the traditional Easter Sunday service, followed by the Royal Easter Egg Hunt at the Castle this afternoon. Edward had his bunny outfit on all day, much to the surprise of the Canon of St George's Chapel. Quite put him off his sermon.

Camilla got the wrong end of the stick and spent the afternoon actually collecting eggs from the Royal Chicken Coops. Still, at least we'll have something for breakfast. Bit of emotion when Andrew's Easter egg count beat Edward's. Edward hopped off in a bit of a temper but one couldn't help but think that the bunny costume somewhat lessened the drama. Turns out that

Andrew had been saving the eggs up from last year's hunt. He's a competitive little sod. Sent the corgis out to see if they could find Edward and tell him the good news.

As is traditional for the Supreme Governor of the Church of England and Defender of the Faith at Easter, one ended the day with a gin and tonic and an Easter egg the size of a Rugby ball.

- MONDAY 25TH APRIL, 2011
'The Middletons are here. They've brought an ASDA "bumper value box of meat". Awkward. Very awkward.'

Easter Monday and Royal Wedding Week. Settling down to breakfast in the garden room at Windsor Castle when a giant pink rabbit hopped past carrying a basket of Easter eggs. Wondered for a second if one should start to moderate the Royal gin intake but soon realised that it was Edward. He'd been up all night after yesterday's Royal Easter Egg Hunt, searching for the last remaining egg. Must be boiling in that bunny outfit.

Having the Middletons over this afternoon for a pre-wedding BBQ. The DoE has lit the second biggest fire one has ever seen (the first was when St George's Hall burned down) and a couple of footmen are roasting an entire pig on the spit.

The Middletons arrived a little after 2 p.m. with an ASDA 'bumper value box of meat' and a case of Fosters. Awkward. Spent a good hour trying to identify the various cuts of meat before the DoE suggested we pop them in the freezer for the next time Mr Cameron comes round. The Fosters went down better, although by 7 p.m. the DoE had consumed the lot and gone for a walk around Windsor. Luckily someone found him, wrote 'Windsor Castle' on his forehead and popped him in a taxi, so all's well that ends well.

Mr Middleton said the castle was a lot bigger than it looked on the telly and asked if one had

had it valued recently. One said there was a limited market for a thousand year old castle with a thousand rooms and that one thought it was probably listed. He said he knew a good estate agent if one were ever interested.

• TUESDAY 26TH APRIL, 2011

'One can confirm that there will be a fruitcake at the wedding. In fact, there will be two as Mr Cameron is also bringing Mr Clegg.'

The Royal Wedding preparations are in full swing. One spent the morning on the seating plan. Popped the Spencer family on the bride's side; they always seemed more comfortable with that. Managed to get Mr Cameron and Mr Clegg behind a floral display with severely restricted view (meaning that they should be almost invisible to the entire congregation). The DoE said they'd probably want some 'private time' anyway. Managed to get Victoria Beckham a few more rows back, just behind the waiting staff.

Polished off the last of the Easter eggs. Elton John called (again) to suggest a last minute rewrite of 'Candle in the Wind' might be appropriate for the wedding – changing 'goodbyes' to 'hellos' etc. Said he had his own piano and PA system and everything and could bring it all in his van. One assured him that it was not necessary on this occasion or approximately any other Royal occasion he could come to think of. He seemed happy with that.

• WEDNESDAY 27TH APRIL, 2011
'Text from Mr Clegg: "Just seen the horses on the TV! Did I miss it?!! I thought it was Friday. SO stupid!"'

Wednesday already and back to Buckingham Palace. William looks as nervous as a Yorkshire Terrier. Last dress rehearsal this morning – the horses were out before dawn. Mr Clegg texted to say he'd seen the horses on the TV and apologised for missing the big day. One didn't respond in the hope that he might actually not turn up on Friday.

Edward emerged at about 10.30 a.m. in the most
beautiful frock. Poor chap had got the wrong idea
about 'dress rehearsal' but there was no denying
that he looked a picture. He thought no point getting
changed just for the sake of it and stayed in costume
all day, leaving a trail of sequins behind him.

Quick one-to-one with Mr Cameron in the afternoon.
He always looks so uncomfortable standing up
but one reminded him that, in the spirit of national
savings, one had cut back on the number of
available chairs in the Palace. He talked for a while
about how much of a good job he was doing and said
what a great feeling there was in the country that
two people were so much in love. Wasn't entirely
sure if he was talking about William and Catherine
or himself and Mr Clegg, but one smiled and
nodded and pressed the eject button to summon a
couple of footmen to come and remove him.

Finalised the wedding playlist. Lots of Queen.
Obviously. William had requested some Prince.
Gin and bed.

● Thursday 28th April, 2011

'Packed one's handbag for tomorrow's wedding (miniature gin, remote weapons button, reading glasses, iPhone, bag of peanuts).'

Up with the cock. Busy day ahead. Throwing a dinner for fifty Heads of State tonight, followed by a general telling-off for their collective sodding up of the world.

Packed one's handbag for the wedding: miniature gin, remote weapons button, reading glasses, iPhone and a bag of peanuts. Essentially, everything a twenty-first century monarch needs to maintain global security. The DoE spent the entire day in a Tony Blair mask, which he wanted to wear to the wedding. One couldn't deny that the look on Mr Cameron's face would be worth it but didn't think that the press would get the joke.

Final review of the guest list. Decided to bar the Syrian Ambassador. Mr Cameron said that politicians oppressing their people simply couldn't attend, but changed his mind when one pointed out that would include him and his entire Cabinet.

Had the Heads of State over for a pre-wedding dinner in the evening. Slightly embarrassing: Sheikh Ahmad Hmoud Al-Sabah of Kuwait got stuck in the loo. Poor chap was in there for half an hour before calling for help. Awkward. Luckily the Grand Duke of Luxembourg had a screwdriver on him (although why one may never know) and the Sheikh rejoined the party without too much commotion. Camilla said she'd had problems with the lock on that door too. It apparently eases up a little if one holds a cigarette lighter under it for a bit.

One does enjoy having foreign royals round. Andrew said he hasn't seen this many queens since that party at Elton John's. The King and Queen of Norway headed off early to Westminster Abbey with a sleeping bag at about

8ish. Wanted to get a good seat and not afraid of the cold, apparently. The King of Tonga did his usual table dance, which caused a bit of a stir, but otherwise all went smoothly.

Midnight: The footmen have managed to stop Prince Albert II of Monaco singing. He does like to put on a bit of a show for the ladies. One's housemaids were beside themselves with excitement, by all accounts.

2 a.m.: Settled down with *The Beano* and a sweet sherry nightcap.

• **FRIDAY 29TH APRIL, 2011**
'Someone have Phillip Schofield sent over here. The Queen of Spain is beside herself with excitement.'

Wedding day. All started off a bit chaotic at the Palace. King Simeon II of Bulgaria insisted on cooking everyone breakfast, which was kind, and the Crown Prince of the Netherlands emerged wearing what one can only describe as an 'alternative' outfit. Sent him upstairs to change immediately – he's not going to Westminster Abbey wearing that and that is the end of it.

The Queen of Spain spent the entire morning trying to catch a glimpse of Phillip Schofield through the Palace windows. She loves that man. One offered to have him oiled and sent over but she said she'd feel awkward before lunch. We were all soon distracted by Princess Maha Chakri Sirindhorn of Thailand smoking the biggest cigar one has ever seen and the DoE and the Crown Prince of Abu Dhabi leading a Dolly Parton singalong of foreign royals in the ballroom, including quite an impressive version of 'Baby I'm Burning'. Really should get them together more often.

Hat on at the last minute (the Queen of Denmark had been trying to see it all morning so she could nip out and place a bet on the colour with Camilla) and sent a Rolls-Royce over to pick up Catherine. It was the car that the Prince of Wales trashed by having it driven through the centre of the student protests earlier in the year. Hopefully this time the police might stop the crowds getting too close. Can't have Catherine being poked with a stick. Camilla hasn't been the same since.

The DoE popped the foreign royals on a bus to the Abbey and waved them off. Couldn't help but think that they looked like the Cliff Richard Fan Club on a day trip to Royal Ascot. Jumped in the Bentley a little while later and made the short trip to Westminster. Thought, as one drove past the screaming crowds, that all this will be William's one day. He's a good boy. One hopes it all works out well for him.

Arrived at the Abbey, had a few choice words with the Dean of Westminster, flicked the Royal iPhone to silent and settled down for the service. You'd have thought someone might have put a softer cushion on one's chair.

Major seating plan error. While Mr Cameron and Mr Clegg were virtually hidden from the entire congregation and unable to see anything of the service, they were in one's direct line of sight. Not sure how one managed to miss that. And one does wish Nick Clegg would stop winking at me. Spent most of the service feeling slightly awkward about Princess Beatrice's hat, to be honest. Suggested she get rid of it on eBay. It was all over in a flash and we headed back to the Palace for a well deserved Gin O'Clock.

The foreign Royals followed in their little minibuses and after a few gin cocktails and cheese straws it was out on the balcony for the obligatory appearance. One does like these moments: flag-waving people as far as the eye can see. The RAF did a spectacular fly-past, before heading over to the Continent to fire a few warning shots at France. The crowds were chanting 'kiss, kiss, kiss' at William and Catherine. Told the DoE not to get any ideas.

Back inside for a quick spot of lunch and a Queen medley. One does wish the King of Tonga wouldn't do that thing while he's eating but one doesn't like to say anything in case it's some kind of religious ritual. Moment of panic when one caught sight of Mr Blair on the lawn. Thankfully, popped one's glasses on before giving the 'shoot' order and realised it was Mr Cameron looking for a Portaloo. False alarm.

Decided to leave them to it and headed off in the Royal helicopter for a quiet weekend with the DoE and a few celebratory gins. The Pope texted to say he'd 'watched the whole thing on TV. You looked A-MAZ-ING. Love, love, love that hat!', which was nice.

Headed to bed approximately ¾ full of gin, ¼ full of wedding cake and 100 per cent full of happiness. God Save One. And God bless William and Catherine.

Items to sell on eBay

1. Princess Beatrice's Royal Wedding hat
2. Set of coasters from the Pope
3. Signed copy of Mrs Thatcher's memoirs
4. Lord Sugar
5. France

The Eurovision Song Contest, State Visit to Ireland and State Visit by the Obamas

Agenda:
Meeting with the Irish President

1. Loan repayment
2. Bono
3. Jedward
4. Loan repayment
5. Loan repayment

- SATURDAY 14TH MAY, 2011
'Get the Queen of the Netherlands on the phone.'

Chorizo baked eggs for breakfast with toast and a pot of tea and the morning papers before heading out for a walk with the corgis. Headed back to the Palace for this evening's Eurovision Song Contest.

One does like the Eurovision Song Contest. It always reminds one how much more civilised the British are than our European neighbours. Royal Eurovision Fancy Dress Party to celebrate. Edward was in costume early. One has never seen so many sequins. He does look lovely. Virtually indistinguishable from Gina G. The DoE popped out for a case of gin, saying he'll be 'making his mind up' about cocktails, much to his own amusement.

Beatrice and Eugenie came as Jedward, which was quite convincing, to be fair to them. Unfortunately the Duchess of Cornwall misread the invitation as 'Eurotunnel Fancy Dress Party' and came as a train. Awkward.

Germany are hosting, and one cannot help but think that they do this kind of thing exceptionally badly. The Kaiser would never have allowed it.

Denmark was up first, and Queen Margrethe II was immediately on the phone, convinced it was a winning song. The DoE told her to sod off. It's at moments like this that one is reminded why the United Kingdom is physically and emotionally separate from Europe.

Thoroughly embarrassing Irish attempt. Even the corgis got up and left the room. Made a note to mention this in Ireland next week. Must be very awkward for them. The DoE said it was clear that they were culturally bankrupt too. Sweden's entry managed to sink even lower though. King Carl XVI Gustaf texted to say, 'Sorry about this, Your Majesty. This is very embarrassing.' What a difference a few years without Abba can make.

One can't help but think that Estonia has deep-rooted social problems.

The Greek entry was very difficult. Proof, as if any was needed, of what happens in countries that abandon their monarchy. Followed by the French. Constitutionally speaking, one simply cannot abide the French, although one is of course still technically Queen of France. Text President Sarkozy but he said he wasn't watching, which was clearly a lie.

While one always finds it almost impossible to watch Eurovision without feeling so very lucky to have been born in Britain, the UK entry was admittedly very awkward. Edward was in tears. He's such a Blue fan and was so excited that they'd reformed, but their performance really did go rather badly. The DoE didn't help: he texted Graham Norton to ask, 'What's blue and can't sing? Blue.' Edward didn't find it funny. Sequins everywhere. No idea where he went.

For some reason, the Moldavians decided that pointy hats were the order of the day. Does everyone in Moldova have a pointy head? The DoE says he's ordering a pointy hat for next week's Ireland visit.

Things are obviously very difficult in Austria.

Spain had hardly sung a note when the Queen of Spain called, wondering if Phillip Schofield would like it. One's promised to have him sent over as a host if they win.

Quite amazed at what is clearly a very difficult social problem in Georgia. Considered for a minute sending troops in to break the thumb and forefinger of anyone attempting to sing, but Prime Minister Putin called to say he had it under control.

Well, no surprises that the UK didn't fare well in the voting. David Cameron texted to say that this is what happens with the AV system. Mr Clegg said it was an example of why first past the post is only suitable for entertainment shows.

Two points from Iceland. One is not knocking
that off their three billion pound banking crisis
bill. Sent a text to tell them to get fishing and to
remind them that volcanic ash is not a substitute
for cash. Bloody hell, who'd have thought
Azerbaijan would win?! The DoE thought it only
existed in children's books.

Downed a gin and retired safe in the knowledge
that we have retained moral, cultural, intellectual
and military superiority over the Europeans.

• MONDAY 16TH MAY, 2011
'It's just another manic Monday.'

Off to Ireland tomorrow for one's first ever
visit. Having bought it during the banking
crisis, one thought that it was about time
one popped over and provided a bit of Royal
Guidance in person. Besides which, the DoE
has always wanted to go. And there are the
Bono and Jedward problems to address. Plus
the loan repayment, of course.

Mr Cameron has announced he's coming over too. If there is one thing certain about politicians it's that they do love to hang on one's coat tails and hope a bit of monarchical magic might reflect on them. One made it clear that we are not travelling 'in coalition'.

Slightly awkward conversation with the Irish President. She'd apparently thought that one was bringing Simon Cowell, not David Cameron. One hates to disappoint. Googled Ireland to see how far it was. Surprisingly close. Just next door, in fact.

Mr Clegg texted to ask if, seeing as Mr Cameron and I are in Ireland, that meant he was in charge. No. Quite frankly one wouldn't leave Mr Clegg in charge of a water pistol let alone a Government. Assured him that fifteen overseas territories would attest that one does not have to be present to be in charge and that one would be keeping an eye out for any sodding around while one was debt collecting across the Irish Sea.

Midnight: Had a quick gin and packed one's handbag for the trip: anti-Bono spray, earplugs, iPhone, miniature gin. The DoE downed a few pints of Guinness 'to get in the mood' and we headed to bed.

• TUESDAY 17TH MAY, 2011

'You're not wearing that, Philip. One doesn't care how funny you'd find the look on their faces.'

Off to Ireland today. The DoE emerged wearing a costume from *Riverdance*. Told him he wasn't wearing that, no matter how funny he'd find the look on their faces. Camilla texted to say, 'Charles said you're going to Iceland; can you pick me up some frozen prawns and a box of those Yorkshire puddings?' One didn't reply.

Decided against taking an RAF plane of the Queen's Flight. They're a bit sensitive about seeing British military aircraft landing in Dublin, apparently. Had considered booking Ryanair but apparently the Dublin planes land in Wales and there's a connecting ferry, so one chartered a little plane from British Airways instead.

Arrived to a warm welcome. It's quite nice over here actually. Decided on a green coat and hat, as only a loving and gracious Queen would. The DoE said one looked like a leprechaun, but they seemed to appreciate it. No sooner had we arrived at the Irish President's residence than the DoE broached the Jedward subject. Awkward. After what seemed like an eternity of silence, the President agreed that they were an Irish national embarrassment.

Moved onto loan repayment terms. One had to make the point that Louis Walsh was not sufficient loan security. After much discussion, including the possibility of making the Duke of York Governor-General, the Irish President agreed to repay the loan quick-smart and said if it wasn't settled before one's Diamond Jubilee she would completely understand if one had to put the country on eBay.

Final subject before heading out to greet the people: Bono. After much discussion we agreed a historic treaty that would bring an end to him as a legal entity and therefore spare one's subjects on both sides of the Irish Sea from his self-righteous outpourings. Texted Nelson Mandela the good news. The poor chap has been stalked by Bono for years and apparently at times has almost resorted to going back to prison to get away from him.

Changed out of the green and into a white number for a tour of Dublin. It's tough being a fashion Queen. One's been colour-blocking for decades.

11 p.m.: Having repaired more than a hundred years of troubles, one settled down for a gin-enhanced Guinness and a singsong of Irish folk music.

• WEDNESDAY 18TH MAY, 2011
'Got one's swag on.'

Day two of one's Irish trip. Got one's swag on and headed down for breakfast. To one's absolute dismay they'd laid on a selection of cold meats, some croissants and jam and a bowl of fruit. One day the Euro, the next this. One politely declined and asked if they had any bacon and tomato sauce, which thankfully they did. A Queen can't reign on a croissant. One only has to look to France and Marie Antoinette for proof of that. The DoE is convinced that if she'd had a better breakfast she'd have never ended up going to the guillotine. Ridiculous form of capital punishment, incidentally.

Decided to give the Irish a day off as only a hereditary monarch can. Mr Cameron is coming over today to share the Royal limelight. Had to explain to the Irish President who he was. She asked if he was bringing the children, but one said Mr Clegg and Mr Osborne were staying in London as they have ballet on a Wednesday.

More sights and sounds of Ireland before heading back to get ready for this evening's State Dinner. The Duchess of Cornwall called to ask if one could bring back a case of Guinness. She's a bit partial to the black stuff, apparently. She said that the corgis were fine but that she was a bit worried about the Cabinet. Told her to give them each a biscuit and a kick in the arse if they started playing up. She said she would and that she may well use the same technique with the corgis.

Decided against wearing the Imperial State Crown to the State Dinner. One doesn't like to intimidate small countries by wearing more diamonds than they have people. Started one's speech in Irish, which turned out to be something of a Royal diplomatic coup. Finished the evening feeling most pleased to have gone some way towards putting the wrongdoing and bad feelings of the past behind our respective countries and feeling positive for our future as neighbours. Everybody needs good neighbours, as they like to say in Australia.

• THURSDAY 19TH MAY, 2011
'Good gracious, it's gone Gin O'Clock!'

Day three of one's Irish trip. Up early, this time thankfully to a proper breakfast. One has got to hand it to the Irish: they make a pretty good bacon sandwich when they set their minds to it. And they're fast learners: not a croissant in sight.

Suggested to the Irish PM that now the continental breakfast has gone he might have a rethink about the Euro. He said he couldn't for the life of him understand why they have fought against such good British advice in the past. One took that as a compliment.

Another day of smiling and nodding. If this doesn't get us twelve points from Ireland at next year's Eurovision Song Contest, one doesn't know what will.

• Friday 20th May, 2011
'Well, that went well. Flying back to Blighty for an immediate Gin O'Clock.'

Final day of one's Irish trip. Seems to have gone well so far. Mr Cameron has gone back to London a day early as Mr Clegg has apparently already had a disastrous impact on economic growth and has all but stripped the downstairs loo at Downing Street of wallpaper.

Off to Tipperary today. The DoE said it was a long way to Tipperary, a long, long way to go, but one didn't think it was all that far. And finally some sunshine. One was starting to think that it was a constant washout in Ireland.

8 p.m.: Having got Ireland broadly back on track, one headed home for a constitutional amount of gin and *Gardeners' World* with Monty Don. He's got nothing on Geoff Hamilton but one supposes the BBC have to make do.

- MONDAY 23RD MAY, 2011
'Tell one why one don't like Mondays, tell one why one don't like Mondays. One wants to sho-oooooo-ot the whole day down.'

Up at the crack of dawn, as usual. One sometimes wonders what Queen Victoria was thinking when she instructed a lone piper to play outside her window at such ungodly hours. Still, one doesn't like to make unnecessary changes, and if nothing else it does mean that in almost sixty years one has never been late to rule.

Started off the day with a bacon sandwich. Busy week coming up: Iceland is sending over an ash cloud and America is sending over the Obamas. Sent a message to the Icelandic Government to remind them that one hasn't forgotten the three billion they owe and suggested that they might want to attach some cash and send that over as well. No response.

Irish President Mary McAleese texted to say 'Obama has NOTHING on you, Your Majesty. He didn't even wear a hat!' Quite. Can't for the life of me understand why Mr Obama is coming via Ireland in the first place. The DoE thinks he's probably flying Ryanair to London, which apparently lands in Dublin before a 'short bus ride' for the remainder of the route. It's not often that one conducts American-president annual appraisals in person but he seems keen to come and Mr Clegg is just dying to meet him.

3 p.m.: Rounded off the afternoon with a few G&Ts at the Chelsea Flower Show. Wandered into the Wallflower Garden and thought for a moment that one might have stumbled into a Liberal Democrat conference.

• TUESDAY 24TH MAY, 2011
'No, President Obama, you cannot "pop over earlier"; one has a Commonwealth to rule and is on something of a schedule.'

That bloody lone piper. Obama has landed early, thanks to the Icelandic ash cloud. He sent a text asking if he could pop over early as he was at something of a loose end. The DoE replied to say 'sod off'. Sending Charles and Camilla over to pick them up. Edward wanted to go but one's keeping him at home and topped up with dolly mixtures.

Camilla texted to say: 'It's Obama! I thought you said "go and collect a llama". I brought a packet of peanuts and everything.' That must have been a shock. Still, one hopes the peanuts helped to coax them out of the American Embassy. Come to think of it, it was the only way one could persuade Gordon Brown to leave Downing Street in the end.

Had a few hundred armed troops lined up on the Palace lawn to remind the Obamas what failing a probation review with the monarch looks like, then whisked them inside to meet William and Catherine. Michelle Obama asked Catherine if she was looking forward to judging American *X Factor*, which was a bit awkward but we went with it. Popped them in their ridiculous armed limo and sent them off for an afternoon with the Camerons with strict instructions to be back for Gin O'Clock at 5 p.m., and had a little disco nap before the State Banquet.

Bit embarrassing. Mr Clegg arrived a full three hours early for dinner (said he wanted to get a good seat) and Mr Obama mistook him for a footman. One assured Mr Obama that the quality of footmen in this palace is much, much higher than that. Queen Mary always said that arriving early was worse manners than arriving late. Still, Mr Clegg did come in handy in the kitchen: there were hundreds of potatoes to peel.

State Banquet went well, although Mr Obama did manage to mess up the toast. Camilla was practically wetting herself but one managed to smile politely as if nothing had happened. The DoE suggested afterwards that a few hundred years of independence had clearly had a seriously diminishing effect on manners. Luckily he was talking to a statue by mistake, so no offence caused.

Formalities out of the way and on to State Karaoke in the ballroom. Notable performances from:

- Tony Blair: 'I Will Survive' (which struck one as deeply ironic)
- David Cameron and Nick Clegg: 'Wind Beneath my Wings' (under duress from the

DoE but they seemed to enjoy it once they got into it. Though one thought the hand-holding a little over the top)

- Mr Obama: 'Bohemian Rhapsody' (with Camilla on air guitar)
- Oneself: 'Killer Queen' (which served as entertainment as well as a warning)

The DoE wanted to do 'American Idiot', convinced that it would be worth it for the look on Hillary Clinton's face, but one managed to restrain him. Not entirely sure what happened to Camilla. She'd put her name down for 'American Trilogy' but didn't turn up. Last seen on the terrace wrapped in the Stars and Stripes and smoking a cigar the size of a marrow, apparently.

- WEDNESDAY 25TH MAY, 2011
'Denmark has banned Marmite. Seriously considering banning Denmark.'

The piper had barely blown a note when one was woken by loud American voices. Mr Obama was up at the crack of dawn and insisted on making everyone pancakes. One doesn't like to be rude but would have much preferred a bacon sandwich. And besides which, that's not a pancake, and whatever it is there is no need to soak it in syrup. Really, one does wonder how they've managed without a monarchy all these years.

Popped the Obamas in the car for a day of boosting British political egos and settled down to the news that Denmark has banned Marmite. Seriously considering banning Denmark. Margrethe II called to apologise and said she was sorting it quick-smart. One actually cannot stand Marmite but one's not having the Danish take the culinary upper hand. The DoE says they're still upset that British bacon has come so far.

Dinner at the American Embassy to tell Mr Obama he'd passed his annual appraisal but would remain on probation for approximately eternity. Quite tempted to talk through his National Anthem, as he'd talked through ours, but resisted.

Back to the Palace for a martini, a packet of Mini Cheddars and bed.

- **THURSDAY 26TH MAY, 2011**
'Cheryl Cole on the phone. Can't understand a word she's saying.'

Up with the piper to make sure that Immigration had successfully removed the Obamas. Had to physically carry Mr Obama onto the plane apparently. Bowl of Coco Pops and a pot of tea before reviewing the Government's latest ridiculous ideas in the State Papers. Really, one sometimes wonders if direct rule would be simpler. Have asked one's private secretary to look into it.

Settled down to lunch when Cheryl Cole called. Absolutely no idea what she was talking about. The DoE said she had been sacked from American *X Factor* as the Americans were having trouble understanding her accent. Not surprised: one had an entire phone conversation with her once before realising one was listening to a car alarm. Michelle Obama sent a message to say how upset she was that Catherine wouldn't be on American *X Factor* any more.

4.30 p.m.: Took the corgis out for a walk before Gin O'Clock and faced the undeniable truth that it was absolutely pissing with rain. Sheltered for a while in the Buckingham Palace gift shop and bought a pack of postcards and a Prince of Wales teddy bear.

• FRIDAY 27TH MAY, 2011
'Who can take a sunrise, sprinkle it with dew?
Cover it with chocolate and a miracle or two? The
Sovereign . . . Ooo the Sovereign can . . .'

Managed to drown out the piper with Radio 2. Sausage sandwich in bed listening to Chris Evans, who happily had Brian May and Roger Taylor from Queen with him. If there is one regret in one's long reign, it's not knighting Freddie Mercury. Got quite carried away and nearly forgot to rule Jamaica.

The Archbishop of Canterbury popped round for afternoon tea. Not sure what it is about that man but the corgis are always on edge when he's around. He thinks it's his aura. The DoE says he should 'leave his bloody aura at the door'. After an hour of supreme governing, ecclesiastical steering and religious motivation one popped him on his bicycle and called Gin O'Clock.

Royal iPhone to silent and an evening of *Miss Marple* DVDs.

The DoE's 90th, Official Birthday and Honours, Ascot, and William and Catherine in Canada

Draft list of people to be knighted

1. Freddie Mercury (posthumously)
2. Brian May
3. Roger Taylor
4. John Deacon
5. Phillip Schofield
6. Hugh Grant

- MONDAY 6TH JUNE, 2011
'Goodness, time for a gin and Dubonnet.'

Woke up at the crack of dawn, took the corgis out before breakfast and promptly got absolutely soaked by the rain. Never ceases to amaze one how England can go from clear blue skies to torrential downpour in approximately thirty seconds. Headed back to the Castle for a bacon sandwich and a blow dry. Rainy days and Mondays always get one down.

The Business Secretary, Vince Cable, called about mid-morning. Something about strikes and how one doesn't pay any attention to him. Wasn't really listening, to be honest. Told him to call back after *This Morning* but he never did. One's promised the Queen of Spain Phillip Schofield for Christmas and has started watching *This Morning* intently to decide how one might wrap him. The DoE thinks he'd look nice with a bow.

Mrs 'no really, call me Carole' Middleton called after lunch. She says, 'us mums and grannies should catch up once a week'. Popped her on hold while she gave the obligatory 'online party accessories' business update and raided the kitchen for a packet of Fruit Pastilles. She was still chatting away when one got back. Ordered some 'value bunting' to keep her happy and was dismayed to see that the postage and packing cost almost ten times as much as the bunting itself. No wonder they have a garden big enough for William to land his helicopter.

• TUESDAY 7TH JUNE, 2011
'OK Wales, stand by. Your undoubted Queen and Sovereign Lady is coming over to open the Welsh Assembly.'

7 a.m.: Off to Wales today to open the Welsh Assembly. One decided to call it an 'assembly' as it is actually like addressing a hall full of schoolchildren. Although they never seem

to want to sing a hymn before it starts. Took the helicopter and wondered for a minute about flying on to France and reclaiming it for England. But then it's in a bit of a state and the DoE thinks one really ought to get Ireland sorted first.

The Welsh were very friendly, considering whom they have as their Prince. Gave a short address assuring them that the love of their Queen was equalled only by Her contempt for elected representatives. They seemed to take that well. The DoE suggested that they might have spent some money on the Welsh economy or health service instead of building themselves 'a bloody great building to sit in'. Luckily he's not fab at Welsh and they assumed he was saying he liked the furniture.

Hotfooted it back to London and dropped Apple's Mr Jobs a line. He assured one that one's iRule app would work with his new iCloud thing.

10 p.m.: Finished the day with a traditional Welsh drink of gin and tonic.

● **WEDNESDAY 8TH JUNE, 2011**
'Mr Cameron's here for his weekly ego-realignment. Keeping him waiting while one has a gin and Dubonnet.'

Have decided to have a morning off – or 'reigning in the Solomon Islands' as the DoE calls it. Spent about half an hour catching up on affairs of state in one's Caribbean territories (they all seem to run remarkably well without any discernable sign of a Government) and the rest of the morning knitting the Duchess of Cambridge a hat as William said she was getting a bit chilly up there in the arse end of Wales while he's flying about in his helicopter.

Mr Cameron dropped in after Prime Minister's Questions for his weekly ego-realignment. Kept him waiting while one had a gin and Dubonnet and then asked him exactly the same questions he'd been asked in the House of Commons an hour before. Drives the poor chap mad. He said he wasn't enjoying being prime minister as much as he'd expected to. One assured him that one wasn't enjoying him being prime minister either and, judging by the letters one receives from one's subjects, neither were they. Popped him back in his car with a few choice words of regal advice and rushed back in to catch the end of *Ready Steady Cook*. Never ceases to amaze one what those chefs can do with a tin of corned beef, a carrot and a jar of pickles.

• THURSDAY 9TH JUNE, 2011
'Up early for a pre-reign bacon sandwich.'

Woken at the crack of dawn by a Lady in Waiting. Her watch had apparently stopped at 8 p.m. the evening before and she rushed in thinking one might have overslept. One explained that it was in fact 4.30 a.m. and dispatched her to make one a bacon sandwich by way of apology.

Spent most of the day preparing for the DoE's birthday tomorrow. Have ordered the most enormous cake. Camilla is going to burst out of it, covered head to toe in sequins. Took all morning to explain to Edward all the reasons why it was inappropriate for him to do it.

Mr Clegg called after lunch to say he was deeply disappointed not to have made the Rear of the Year list again. One assured him that the DoE thinks he is a perfect arse. He said he would campaign for the Alternative Vote system next year as he's convinced that will boost his chances no end. As far as one can see, the poor man is pinning his hopes of any kind of victory from here on in to people being unable to decide between politicians they might actually like.

Settled down for an evening in front of the TV with the DoE and we were both amazed to see Fiona Bruce interviewing him. We thought she'd only come over to value him for the

Antiques Roadshow. Poor thing didn't seem to be coping well with the interview. The Prince of Wales says she must now realise why he's known colloquially as the Duke of Hazard. Still, one had hoped he'd be worth at least £250 but she didn't even get an expert to value him.

● FRIDAY 10TH JUNE, 2011
'Happy Birthday DoE, Happy Birthday DoE, Happy Birthday Duke of Edinburgh, Happy Birthday DoE . . .'

It's the DoE's 90th birthday! Day full of surprises, starting with Brian May playing a guitar solo rendition of 'Happy Birthday' standing on the breakfast table. Can't wait to see his face when Camilla jumps out of the cake at lunchtime. The Department of Education called; apparently Mr Clegg had sent them a 90th birthday card and they rather thought it might have been meant for the DoE. Awkward.

Have decided to take Queen Anne's lead and make the DoE Lord High Admiral for his 90th. Although, on hearing the announcement, Mr Clegg was straight on the phone asking if that meant he was automatically Deputy Lord High Admiral. He apparently already has the outfit and a dinghy on the Downing Street pond. One said that he could be if he could get from Downing Street to open water without crossing land. He said he'd get to it right away. Should keep him out of Mr Cameron's hair for a while.

Birthday lunch, followed by the cake. We all stood round waiting expectantly for a sequin-clad Camilla to emerge like an apparition but there was no sign of her. The catering company called to say they'd accidently popped her in the wrong cake and that she'd inadvertently ruined a five year old's birthday party in Stoke Newington. Awkward.

Disco nap in the afternoon before the main event: the DoE's 90th Birthday Tarts and Vicars Fancy Dress Party. The Archbishop of Canterbury, rather predictably, came as a Vicar. Edward came as all of the characters from *The Rocky Horror Picture Show* rolled into one. Camilla finally made it back from Stoke Newington but sadly got the wrong end of the stick and came dressed as an apple tart. Still, we all like a bit of custard.

• SATURDAY 11TH JUNE, 2011
'Happy Official Birthday to me, Happy Official Birthday to me, Happy Official Birthday my Majesty, Happy Official Birthday to me.'

Official Birthday! There aren't many perks of being the monarch of sixteen sovereign nations, Head of the Commonwealth, Supreme Governor of the Church of England, Defender of the Faith, Duke of Normandy, Lord of Man, Duke of Lancaster and Paramount Chief of Fiji, but having two birthdays is one of them.

The DoE and the family gathered about the Royal Bed for a chorus of 'Happy Official

Birthday' and one got to work opening one's cards and presents. The Irish President had sent £250 as an early debt instalment, which was nice, and a copy of Jedward's new song, which wasn't.

The Birthday Honours have been announced, including:

- Bruce Forsyth has been made a knight on the strict understanding he seriously reduce his TV appearances and ditch the ridiculous toupee
- Colin Firth has been made a CBE for his portrayal of one's father in *The King's Speech*
- Mr Clegg, the Deputy Prime Minister, gets a Blue Peter Badge for his painting
- Bryan Ferry has been made a CBE for singing at Edward's birthday party for twenty consecutive years
- BBC Radio 4 presenter Jenni Murray has been made a dame for repeatedly making politicians feel uncomfortable and sound stupid

- Brooke Kinsella has been made an MBE for leaving *EastEnders*
- Andrew Strauss and Alastair Cook are made MBEs for services to cricket (although this may be revoked)
- Lee Westwood has been made an OBE for services to golf and Prince Andrew
- The Governor of the Bank of England has been made a knight for services to one's Royal Ascot cashflow and for keeping interest rates low since one purchased Ireland on a tracker mortgage
- Former Conservative leader Michael Howard has been made a Companion of Honour for failing to win a general election and therefore saving one's people untold suffering
- DJ Bob Harris has become an OBE for playing copious amounts of Dolly Parton
- Children's Laureate Julia Donaldson is made an MBE as Mr Osborne likes her poems

Bruce Forsyth texted to say 'Didn't I do well? Nice to Knight me, to Knight me nice.' Having him downgraded to an MBE. That is too much. And if he breaks his promise and hosts another series of *Strictly Come Dancing* one will have the MBE downgraded to a Blue Peter Badge.

Had an official bacon sandwich for breakfast before getting ready for Trooping the Colour. The DoE came down dressed as an 'official pantomime dame' (said it was a tribute to one's Birthday Honours). Sent him back up to get changed. Lord High Admiral or not, one's not sitting next to him in a carriage when he's looking like Christopher Biggins.

It's a short carriage ride down the Mall to Horse Guards Parade. Thankfully it didn't piss with rain but one brought an official brolly just in case. William joined Charles and Anne on horseback for the first time this year. He looked very fetching in his bearskin. Catherine joined Prince Harry in a carriage with Charles and Camilla and had to endure a full fifteen minutes of him pleading for Pippa Middleton's bottom's phone number.

Mr and Mrs Middleton insisted on taking part and spent the morning in a carriage driving around the gardens of Buckingham Palace. Still, shouldn't be too harsh – they did give one a discount on union flags for the Mall as one ordered them online.

One enjoyed the usual spectacle of military music and stamping. One's request for some Queen went unheeded once again though. It's hard to march to the tune of 'Bohemian Rhapsody', apparently. Something about all the key changes. One had sent them a DVD of Queen at Wembley to show them how Freddie Mercury managed, but perhaps it got lost in the post. One would have thought they might have at least managed 'Super Trooper' in the circumstances, but apparently not.

Took a few snaps on the official Royal iPhone of the amassed soldiers and texted them to President Sarkozy as a warning. Poor chap apparently thought they were arriving in Paris and was halfway to Switzerland before his private secretary managed to catch up with him. He texted to say he wasn't really fleeing and had just fancied an impromptu weekend away.

Back to the Palace for a quick official gin and some official cocktail sausages before the customary balcony appearance. Happily waving when one noticed out of the corner of one's eye Edward with a giant feather in his hat. Awkward.

In for a late long lunch, an official bottle of gin and an official afternoon disco nap. Woke in time to watch *The Cube* on ITV. The Queen of Spain texted to ask 'what one has to do to get in that cube with Phillip Schofield and does it have curtains?'

Camilla came over with a bottle of vodka, having been back to Horse Guards Parade to see if she'd dropped her fags. Couldn't find them anywhere, apparently. Spent almost the entire night in the kitchen making Vesper Martinis (three shots of gin, one shot of vodka, forensically tiny amount of vermouth and a twist of lemon – served ice cold).

Officially virtually preserved in gin.

• SUNDAY 12TH JUNE, 2011
'Australia, take tomorrow off. Your Queen loves you.'

The Governor-General, one's representative in Australia, called at the crack of dawn. They're all feeling a bit left out of the official birthday celebrations, apparently. Assured him that their Queen loved them and said they could all take tomorrow off.

Had poached eggs and muffins with black pudding for breakfast and thumbed through the Sunday papers. The *News of the World* really is awful. Might have it closed at some point. The *Telegraph* ran a lovely front page of one smiling and waving from the Buckingham Palace balcony, standing next to the DoE who, at ninety years old, is still devastatingly handsome. Oh God, it *is* a giant feather in Edward's hat. He must have put it in when one's back was turned. The DoE said he looked like a giant swan.

Settled down for a post-official birthday afternoon of Queen DVDs and a tube of Pringles. Once one pops, one really can't stop. Should really take it a bit easier now that one is officially a year older.

- MONDAY 13TH JUNE, 2011
'Garter Service at Windsor today. John Major's popped in early.'

Up early to prepare for the annual Garter Service at Windsor this morning. Edward is so excited: he does love a hat with a feather (as we discovered at Trooping the Colour). Have invited the Middletons along as William will be in the parade. Mrs 'it's Carole, really' Middleton asked if one wanted her to bring some cheese and

pineapple cocktail sticks for the buffet
afterwards, which was awkward. John Major
popped in early for a bacon sandwich and a
Custard Cream for old time's sake.

Got into the Garter Robes and headed down the
hill to St George's Chapel for the service. William
looked resplendent in his full regalia, although one
couldn't help but notice that Edward had gone a
bit overboard with the feathers. The DoE thought
he looked like a character from *Sesame Street*.

Back up the hill afterwards for a buffet lunch
put on by the Canon of St George's Chapel and a
game of charades. It took the assembled Garter
Knights about three hours to guess Camilla's,
which was ironic as it turned out to be the film
The Queen. She had to resort to pointing at the
Bishop of Reading (all man, one hastens to add,
though one was never entirely convinced about
that other chap they wanted to install there)
before anyone twigged.

Mr Clegg called in the evening to enquire about sharing one's carriage at Ascot tomorrow. Told him one would be delighted and arranged for a footman's uniform to be sent over. One can never have enough footmen, as Queen Victoria used to say.

• Tuesday 14th June, 2011
'Royal Ascot this week. One has decided to stick with the "first past the post" system.'

First day of Royal Ascot today. One does love this time of the year. After the disappointment of the Derby one can feel a winner coming on! Bacon sandwiches all round for brunch and then off to the bookies. One's putting the Irish economy on the first race. Start small. The DoE popped out to put a bet on the colour of one's hat. After a quick Royal Household referendum, one has decided to stick with the first past the post system of selecting a winner.

Hat on and into a carriage for the Royal Procession. It looked distinctly like rain and one did wonder for a second about taking the Bentley down the course but it apparently does nothing for the grass and even less for the suspension. Much cheering and hat waving as we passed the grandstands. Great Britain, your Queen does love you.

Mr Clegg looked a little uncomfortable in his footman's outfit but seemed pleased to have got his wish of sharing one's carriage. One suspects he could have done without that incident with the horse but he managed to clear it all up in no time at all.

6 p.m.: Won absolutely sod all and returned to the Castle for a compensatory gin.

• WEDNESDAY 15TH JUNE, 2011
'The DoE's frying up a full English ahead of today's racing. Just seen one's bookmaker drive past in an Aston Martin.'

Day two of Royal Ascot. Today is the day for winning. The DoE fried up a full English for everyone while one forensically examined the *Racing Post*. Camilla uses the 'pin the tail on the donkey' system for selecting her horses, which seems to serve her well, but we reigning monarchs like to do these things properly.

Cancelled Mr Cameron's weekly audience on account of being busy watching other losers at Ascot. The DoE texted him to say that, unlike him, some horses were capable of actually winning a race. Didn't hear back. Saw one's bookmaker drive past in an Aston Martin on the way to the course. That's always a worrying sign. Who'd have thought the Irish economy would have financed that?

After several very close-run races, one's winnings were marginally less than the absolutely-bugger-all level and one headed back to the Castle for a reassessment of betting formulae and an anaesthetically large gin and tonic.

• THURSDAY 16TH JUNE, 2011

*'Had the Middletons at Ascot today – placing £2.50
each-way bets. Awkward.'*

Day three of Royal Ascot. Absolutely pissing it
down with rain but this is the day for a big win.
The Middletons are coming today, although
one said one would meet them there. One is
purposely avoiding carriage rides with them
after the last time. And to think Mr Middleton
blamed it on the poor horse.

Popped a miniature gin in one's handbag and
headed off for the carriage procession. Hood up
today; it's like midwinter out there.

The Middletons were there waiting and had
been on the champagne since mid-morning by
the look of it. Edward had a quiet word with Mrs
'please call me Carole' Middleton to explain
why the staff weren't curtseying to her. They
seemed to enjoy themselves, although spent
the day placing £2.50 each-way bets, which was

awkward. That said, at the end of the day Mrs 'it's Carole' Middleton had accumulated profits of approximately £28.50 while one had lost a considerable proportion of the Commonwealth economy plus the Solomon Islands.

- **Friday 17th June, 2011**
'Pissing with rain. Again. Having a gin. Again.'

Day four of Royal Ascot. Pissing with rain again. Texted the Archbishop of Canterbury to make an official complaint about the weather. One doesn't ask for much as Supreme Governor of the Church of England but does expect a little bit of sunshine for the races.

The DoE knocked up a round of sausage sandwiches for everyone ahead of the carriage procession. Have invited the Governor of the Bank of England to join us today, although strictly speaking only for reasons of a 'financing bets' nature.

Decided to follow a different strategy today and place everything on the nose of one dead cert horse. Unfortunately it turned out to be the only horse in recent history to fall in a flat race. The Governor of the Bank of England looked deeply troubled but perked up a bit when one authorised a bit of 'quantitative easing' to address the unexpected shortfall.

Headed back to the Castle for an Ascot-themed fancy dress party. Camilla came as a hat. Andrew and Edward came as a horse, although one wasn't sure which end was which.

• SATURDAY 18TH JUNE, 2011
'Approximately ¾ full of gin.'

Final day of Royal Ascot, and historically a big winner. In fact, if one doesn't win today heaven knows what will become of the Solomon Islands. They might even end up in the hands of the French, and one wouldn't wish that on anyone.

Last night's Ascot-themed fancy dress party
went on until the small hours, so there's a
somewhat subdued feeling in the Royal
Household this morning. The DoE made
scrambled eggs with some chilli to perk
everyone up. No idea what happened to Camilla.
She popped out for some 'fresh air' about 1 a.m.
and one hasn't seen her since. She can't have
gone far dressed as a giant hat, presumably.

Arrived slightly late at the racecourse as
Edward had forgotten his Transformers toy
(which he insists on taking everywhere at the
moment) and we had to pop back to the Castle
to collect it. Galloped down the course and
arrived in the Royal Box in time to place the
first bet of the day.

Disappointingly poor performance but managed
to recoup the week's losses with an epic win
on the last race. The DoE had to pop back with
a Range Rover to collect the winnings. The
Governor of the Bank of England will be thrilled,

to say nothing of the people of the Solomon Islands who had been facing a future King Bono.

Finished the day approximately ¾ full of gin, ¼ full of Hula Hoops.

• SUNDAY 19TH JUNE, 2011
'William and Harry got Charles a plastic crown for Father's Day. He's had it on all day.'

Father's Day. Although to be fair to the DoE, he did get up and make one a sausage sandwich and a pot of tea. Having spent almost the entire night celebrating the last minute Ascot win, one awoke this morning to find one's head had been practically Superglued to the pillow.

Father's Day lunch at Windsor. William and Harry got Charles a plastic crown, which he insisted on wearing for the rest of the day. Lady Louisa and Viscount Severn bought Edward a flower press and Princess Beatrice presented Andrew with the proceeds of her eBay Royal

Wedding Hat sale. Charles gave the DoE West Cornwall, which was a lovely gesture.

- **MONDAY 20TH JUNE, 2011**
'Try not to sit down until it clears up, Mr Osborne.'

Back to Buckingham Palace. Had one's private secretary in first thing to catch up on all the gossip. Apparently Mr Osborne hasn't fully recovered from last week's 'incident' but they are hoping the cream will kick in soon. Spent the afternoon reading up on the financial crisis that looks to be engulfing the Euro. Thank God one overruled Mr Blair about joining. Things are always much more secure when embodied by the Queen and this is never more true than in currency.

- **TUESDAY 21ST JUNE, 2011**
'No, one shall not be buying Greece.'

The DoE and I are off to Downing Street today to do some ego-realignment. One rarely makes a visit to the PM but likes to roll the Bentley over every few years to remind them who is in charge. How Mr Cameron copes with such a little house is beyond one, especially now he has his live-in helper (Mr Clegg) and a cat there too.

Arrived around lunchtime. Mrs Cameron managed a curtsey, which is more than Mrs Blair ever did in public. She can't have any knee concerns, clearly. Exchanged pleasantries over lunch before informing Mr Cameron in no uncertain terms that one would not be purchasing Greece, no matter how much debt they'd got themselves into. That country has never been the same since they exiled the DoE.

Mr Clegg made a lovely pot of tea and tapped away on his Fisher-Price 'My First Computer' while the grown ups were talking. If one had known he was going to be there one would have brought Edward and his Transformers toy to keep him amused.

Returned to the Palace about 5ish for an emergency

fourth gin for reasons of a national security nature and had an early night with *Just a Minute* on Radio 4.

- **WEDNESDAY 22ND JUNE, 2011**
'Long conversation with Ms Gillard, one's Australian PM. Can barely understand a word she says. It's very awkward.'

Had a long day ruling Australia and New Zealand. Long conversation with Ms Gillard, one's Australian PM. Can barely understand a word she says if Rolf Harris isn't around to draw a picture to translate. One likes to think of prime-ministerial conversations as an open and frank exchange of views (in that their views are replaced by those of their monarch).

Mr Key (one's New Zealand PM) is much more agreeable. Seriously considering spending more time down there. Might make Charles Governor-General. He loves sheep. And Camilla says she could do with having him out of her hair for a few decades.

Decided to get into the Australasian spirit and invited the Cabinet round for an impromptu BBQ. Vince Cable arrived in shorts and knee-high socks with sandals, which was a bit awkward for everyone. The DoE threw a few burgers on the fire and Camilla buttered some rolls for everyone. All went well until someone stole a sausage from Mr Clegg's plate and he made a bit of a scene. Mr Osborne later owned up and said that he was only planning to put it 'in reserve'. Thankfully Mr Cameron stepped in before all hell broke loose. Had them all shown off the premises at the end of bayonets and settled down for a cold sausage and a few pitchers of Pimm's with the DoE.

• **THURSDAY 23RD JUNE, 2011**
'Bring One's Child to Work Day. Charles is so excited.'

Royal Bring One's Child to Work Day today. Charles arrived at the Palace early, plastic crown and all. Camilla had packed him some sandwiches for lunch. Might let him appoint a few bishops if he's good.

Spent the morning reviewing (rejecting) proposed Government legislation. Charles enacted some ancient residual powers and made it illegal to graze a pig on common land in France on the second Wednesday of each month. Sent a text to President Sarkozy to break the news. He said that the second Wednesday of each month was the last remaining day a Frenchman could graze a pig on common land but didn't seem to think it would be a big problem. Turned one's back for a minute and Charles accidently scrapped the Government's Central Office of Information. Oh well, save a bit of cash at least.

5 p.m.: Ended the day with a mammoth bishop-appointing session. Let Charles dial the numbers but explained that Mummy had to do the talking. He seemed to have fun. One took a photo of him on the throne in his plastic crown for him to take home and show Camilla.

- ## Friday 24th June, 2011
'Great Britain, it's Friday, the sun is shining and your Queen is intensely relaxed about you taking a day off.'

A sunny Friday at last. Sent a message to the population at large and suggested they take the day off. Sent a message to MPs suggesting that they don't.

Hotfooted it back to Windsor for some horse-riding in the Great Park. Interrupted by a phone call from Mrs 'it's Carole' Middleton. Absolutely distraught that Habitat had gone into administration. Said she had been planning on buying a sofabed and did one think she might be able to pick one up in a clearance sale? Popped her on hold and gave the horses a wash down.

Had the Duke and Duchess of Kent over for dinner in the evening. She's gone very quiet since converting to Catholicism.

William is off to Canada tomorrow to see how one's favourite overseas territory is coming along. Told the United Nations that he might pop in on them and give them a bit of direction on his way home. One does enjoy overseas trips and hopes William and Catherine will too. Absence seems to make the heart grow fonder and one's people are always very enthusiastic that their Royals are paying them a visit.

Told William to be packed for all weather eventualities. If there is one thing about Canada it's that one never knows if it's going to be boiling hot or pissing with rain. Much like London in that respect.

Camilla wanted to go along but one explained she is needed in London to keep an eye on Charles. She asked Catherine to pick up some cigarettes in duty free.

• THURSDAY 30TH JUNE, 2011

'Stand by your beds, Canada. The monarchy is coming.'

Have sent William and Catherine off to Canada to keep an eye on Mr Harper. Gave William some notes from one's trip to Canada last year to read on the plane:

William, dear,

You'll be reading this on the plane on the way to Canada. Granny went last year and one thought you might appreciate a bit of a heads-up on a few things.

The Governor General will meet you at the airport. Give a quick speech to say hello. The DoE thinks that doing a bit in French is always well received, but don't overdo it – it makes Mr Sarkozy nervous about a Royal Reclamation of France, and one's subjects in other realms don't like to hear their Royal Family speaking French; they get worried that the Euro is coming or something.

Mr Clegg will probably call you to ask if he is Deputy Prime Minister of Canada as well. He is not. Don't worry if the Canadians don't know who he is; one's trying to keep him a secret for reasons of an international-credibility nature.

You'll probably be asked to conduct a review of one's Canadian Royal Navy. Don't mention this to your Uncle Andrew. He'll be very jealous. You know how he loves dressing up like a sailor. And Camilla called first thing to ask if you would look out for some dry ginger ale. She loves it with a Scotch.

Be prepared: the Canadians are obsessed with asking their Royal Family to plant trees. One's packed you a spade. One felt like Charlie Dimmock by day two. And don't listen to your grandfather; they honestly don't enjoy it when he insists on performing Canadian duties dressed like a Canadian Mountie.

You'll have to spend some time in the French-speaking districts. They never look overly impressed to see their Royal Family in person. Still, one never looks particularly impressed to see

President Sarkozy, so it's probably some sort of karma.

Pop over to America on your way home. When you get there, you might want to pop in on the United Nations. One gave a motivational speech while one was in town last year. The DoE popped over beforehand to remind them that they should have a sovereign standing before them, not a transient two-bit politician. He said they took it well. If you're asked, remember Granny uniquely addresses the United Nations not as Head of State in one country, but as Head of State in sixteen of their nations and as Head of the Commonwealth in many more. You've got all this to come!

Have a good trip. Love to Catherine.

Granny, Queen, Defender etc xx

The Phone Hacking Scandal and the Wedding of Zara Phillips

- ### MONDAY 4TH JULY, 2011

'Mr Obama on the phone for his annual "American Review of Independence Day" conversation with his Queen.'

Up early for American 'Review of Independence Day'. The Americans don't have a wonderful record of post-colonial self-governance, and since George III put them on probation in 1776, successive monarchs have held an annual review. Ordered a bacon sandwich and a pot of sugary tea to build up the energy.

Mr Obama called about 10ish to run through the reasons why they should be allowed a 235th attempt at self-rule, although somewhat defeated his own argument by ending the call begging to be taken back. Decided, after a great deal of thought, to grant continued independence, although warned Mr Obama that they will remain on probation until the end of recorded time. He said he was very grateful and promised to keep Sarah Palin confined to states with sparse populations.

Spent the afternoon looking through the Royal Accounts. Purchasing gin in bulk has paid off: one's expenditure fell by £1.8 million in the last year. Retired with a martini safe in the knowledge that world class monarchical rule is more cost-effective than ever and sent Mr Cameron a quick text to remind him who's in charge.

• TUESDAY 5TH JULY, 2011
'News of the World on the phone. Actually, one was ordering a takeaway but one presumes they were listening in.'

Up with the lark and took the corgis out for a spin around the Buckingham Palace Gardens in an 1812 State Landau. Mr Cameron called to say that he was 'deeply shocked' that phone hacking at the *News of the World* was so widespread. Told him that one was 'deeply shocked' he knew so little about the activities of his best friends and former employees. His mobile signal seemed to deteriorate suddenly and sadly he wasn't able to talk for long.

Asked one's private secretary for a list of the more remote dominions and spent a few hours planning next year's holidays/State Visits. Called the King of Tonga to check that all was well in his neck of the woods, only to find that he still hasn't arrived home from the Royal Wedding. He did say he was going to take the long route. Sent a message to News International to check if he'd left a message on anyone's answerphone. One does hope he's OK. Tonga is one of one's favourite Commonwealth nations, and they do cause one, as their loving overlord, relatively little trouble.

Decided to order takeaway for supper and got straight on the phone to News International. Actually, one was on the phone to Mr Chan from the local Chinese but one expects they were listening in.

- ## WEDNESDAY 6TH JULY, 2011
'The DoE has hacked into Mr Miliband's phone.'

Barely finished one's bacon and eggs when Mr
Clegg turned up at the Palace. Very, very upset that
his phone was not hacked. He says he even gave
Andy Coulson his voicemail PIN and had apparently
left scandalous messages for himself and everything.
One assured him that News International simply
didn't have the technology to hack into a Fisher-
Price mobile and he seemed to relax a little.

Linnet the corgi is very suspicious of Mr Clegg
and has taken to peeing up his leg every time he
arrives at the Palace. The DoE says she's only
doing what we're all thinking, but it is awkward.
One has to receive him in the kitchen as a
precaution. One does find the corgis a good judge
of character though: Monty used to wrestle
Cherie Blair to the floor every time she visited.
Mr Blair called him a 'canine of mass destruction
that could be activated within sixteen minutes'.
One expects the feeling was mutual.

4 p.m.: The DoE has hacked into Ed Miliband's phone. No messages.

- **Thursday 7th July, 2011**
'Pissing with rain. Reigning.'

Absolutely pissing with rain. One got completely soaked walking the corgis through the Palace Gardens and had to take shelter in the Royal Mews gift shop. Spent about an hour surrounded by tourists telling me how much one looked like the Queen. Bought some Buckingham Palace tea towels, a box of Sandringham shortbread and a plastic crown (for Charles' collection) and headed back to take personal charge of clearing up the British media.

Round of cucumber sandwiches and a couple of gin and Dubonnets for lunch before closing the *News of the World*. Gave some serious thought to closing Mr Cameron also but was interrupted by news that Camilla had got lost on her way to open a primary school and had spent the day opening a bottle of gin instead.

One's private secretary popped in to say that he understood Mr Murdoch was considering a Sunday edition of the *Sun*. Assured him that when one said one wanted 'seven days of sun' one was talking about the weather, not another sodding Murdoch paper. God, the *News of the World* was bad enough.

• FRIDAY 8TH JULY, 2011
'Mystic Meg on the phone. One would have thought she'd have seen it coming.'

Thank Crunchie it's Friday. Decided to have a lie-in and reign in Tuvalu from bed. One only has about 10,000 subjects over there so it requires a relatively 'light touch' rule, much like the Liberal Democrats here. Checked on Fiji, New Zealand and Australia while one was in the Pacific Ocean mood and sent one's Australian PM a motivational text message to remind her that one was watching. She hardly ever replies.

Up in time for lunch followed by a quick investiture in the Throne Room. It never ceases to amaze one how many of one's people from all walks of life achieve such wonderful things for their Queen and country. Handing out a few honours is the least one can do. And they always look so thrilled.

Wondered about heading over to Downing Street while one had the sword in one's hand but was interrupted by a call from Mystic Meg. Very upset to lose her job at *News of the World*. Says she didn't see it coming. Poor thing.

Had Andy Coulson arrested, mainly for the embarrassment it would cause Mr Cameron, turned the Royal iPhone to silent and popped on a DVD of *Lock, Stock and Two Smoking Barrels* to watch some criminals doing marginally less harm than the British media.

• SATURDAY 9TH JULY, 2011
'Approximately ¾ full of gin; ¼ full of cheese straws.'

One does enjoy Saturdays. Left the Palace first thing and headed to Windsor. Little wonder Queen Victoria loved this place so much: an Englishman's home is his castle, after all. Quick bacon sandwich for sustenance and went for a ride in the Great Park with the DoE following in a carriage.

Back in time for lunch and a message from the newly constituted South Sudan asking if Prince Edward was available for monarchical duties. Called them back and offered William Hague as Governor-General but they said they thought they'd be able to manage fine on their own, thanks very much. Probably just as well; it would have bankrupted them to keep that forehead properly protected from the sun.

11 p.m.: Sat down after dinner with a bottle of gin, a packet of cheese straws and a Dolly Parton 'Live in London' DVD. The DoE thinks she must be counterbalanced.

- ● SUNDAY 10TH JULY, 2011
'Looking into legislation making it illegal to be Rupert Murdoch in a Commonwealth country.'

Wandered down to St George's Chapel for the Sunday morning service and a Custard Cream with the Canon. Caught up on all the Church of England gossip and gave some ecclesiastical guidance as only a Supreme Governor can.

Arrived back at one's private apartments in time for the British Grand Prix. One had sent Prince Harry to fly the flag, as it were, and he texted to say he was on the starting grid and had 'just met that little Bernie Ecclestone chap. He's tiny'.

Asked one's private secretary to look into what legislation would be required to make it illegal to be Rupert Murdoch in a Commonwealth country. He said he thought it already was.

• MONDAY 11TH JULY, 2011
'The DoE has sold Mr Clegg's mobile number for £2.50.'

One arrived back in London first thing. Took the Royal helicopter to avoid the nightmare M4.

The phone hacking scandal shows no signs of abating. The DoE is taking full advantage and has sold Mr Clegg's mobile number for £2.50, although he suspects the buyer was a proxy for Mrs Clegg, who apparently hasn't seen or heard from him since he moved in with Mr Cameron.

Finalised the menus for tomorrow's garden party at the Palace. Edward's been baking fairy cakes for weeks and thinks he'll have 5,000 ready on time. He's hand-piped a little crown onto the top of each one. Camilla called to check on the dress code and to ask if one wanted her to bring anything (a bottle of wine, some crisps, Charles etc.).

• TUESDAY 12TH JULY, 2011
'Time for a gin. Not you Cameron.'

Garden party at the Palace this afternoon. Apparently tickets are for sale from selected corrupt Royal Protection Police Officers, along with the phone numbers of one's entire family and all garden party guests. There was a queue of journalists at the Palace gates.

One had barely finished laying out the cucumber sandwiches when Mr Clegg called. Bit upset. Apparently one of the knobs on his Etch A Sketch has broken so he can't do any work. The DoE said he was quite sure there were plenty of knobs in Downing Street and that he wasn't looking hard enough if he couldn't find one.

Camilla arrived with a case of gin and a box of duty free cigarettes and joined the DoE and me for the garden party walkabout. Edward's fairy cakes seemed to go down well. Had the gardens cleared about 6ish and headed inside for the evening news. Not sure what happened to Camilla. Perhaps she's still in the fairy cake tent.

• WEDNESDAY 13TH JULY, 2011
'Thinking of making it illegal to be Richard Madeley on radio or TV.'

There is nothing more disappointing in a Queen's life than waking up to find Richard

Madeley standing in for Chris Evans on Radio
2. It really does get one's day off to a bad start.
Popped on a Foo Fighters CD instead and read
the *Racing Post* cover to cover before making yet
another donation to one's bookmaker's Aston
Martin fund.

The Metropolitan Police called to say that the
phone hackers might have listened to Camilla's
voicemails. Called to tell her the bad news
but she seemed quite relieved. Said she's glad
someone has been listening to them; forgot the
PIN number years ago apparently. She sent a
message to *News of the World* to ask if they could
pass on anything urgent and if there had been
any messages from her dry cleaner about that
stain.

Had Mr Cameron over for his weekly
ego-lobotomy in the afternoon, fresh from a
bit of a hard time in the Commons over the
phone hacking. The DoE met him in a Rupert
Murdoch mask, which by all accounts he didn't

find the least amusing. Told him he ought to
be a bit more careful about whom he chooses
as his friends in future and that he might want
to avoid journalists and criminals. He said one
had, as usual, been 'very clear'. One tries one's
best.

Agenda:
Audience with the PM

1. *What value has been added since*
   the general election?

That is all

- **Thursday 14th July, 2011**

'The sun is out, the sky is blue, there's not a cloud to spoil the view and one's reigning. Reigning in one's heart . . .'

Finally some sun. July was starting to look like an Irish summer. Had a couple of sausages and a pot of tea for breakfast, cancelled all appointments and spent the day in the Palace Garden weeding the Busy Lizzies. Mr Clegg popped on his wellies and came to help. He's got a mini-wheelbarrow and spade. It's the most useful thing he's done since being appointed Deputy Prime Minister. Gave him a tomato plant to take back to Downing Street and told him not to plant it in the sandpit.

3 p.m.: Headed to Windsor Castle after supper for a long weekend.

- **Friday 15th July, 2011**

'Great Britain, it is Friday and it is Gin O'Clock. Your Queen loves you.'

Charlie Gilmour (or, as the DoE calls him, 'the little sod who swung from the Cenotaph and hurled a bin at Charles' car') has been jailed. The Duchess of Cornwall is clearing her diary so that she might spend some time poking him with a pointy stick. Or a bayonet. She said she hasn't decided yet.

Mr Murdoch called to say he was sorry about all the phone hacking business. One gave him a few tips on how his sorrow might be more effectively expressed. Must have done the trick as Rebekah Brooks later resigned. The DoE says that's the second red-top to leave News International in the space of a week. Mr Clegg is still deeply upset about the whole thing. Feels he may never get press coverage now he can't even instigate a scandal.

The DoE and I donned a disguise and popped out for dinner at Windsor Royal Station. Sat next to a table of Americans who seemed to be quite taken with the Castle, but said it was such a shame it was built so close to the airport. Sent Mr Obama a quick text.

11.30 p.m.: Back to the Castle for a few press-induced gin and tonics and a box of Turkish Delight. The DoE hacked into the kitchen cupboard and came back with a giant bag of Mini Cheddars, which kept us munching until gone midnight.

- **SATURDAY 16TH JULY, 2011**

'Queen Mother of all hangovers.'

Woke up with the Queen Mother of all hangovers. One's head felt like it had been Superglued to the Royal Pillow again. The DoE got straight on to frying up a full English (fried eggs x 2, grilled tomato, mushrooms, Duchy Originals bacon, Duchy Originals sausages, fried potatoes, baked beans, black pudding, fried bread, toast) and brewed a pot of English breakfast tea to tempt one downstairs. It seemed to soak up most of the excess gin.

Took the corgis out for a quick three hour walk around the Great Park and popped into Fudge

Kitchen on the way back to the Castle. Spent the afternoon with a James Bond DVD box set and box of fudge.

Didn't win the lottery. Again. Bollocks.

- Sunday 17th July, 2011
'Decided to have Rebekah Brooks arrested, for misspelling "Rebecca", if nothing else.'

Quiet day at Windsor so decided to have Rebekah Brooks arrested. Mr Cameron called to say how appalled he was at the whole phone hacking scandal, how he was completely supportive of bringing News International to account and how his Government was absolutely determined to sort it out (it's not his Government, actually, it's mine but one didn't like to interrupt).

Had a spot of lunch and decided to have a sort out at the Met, starting with the Commissioner, Sir Paul Stephenson. Had one's press secretary (not a former *News of the World* employee, unusually) draft his resignation and fax it over for him to sign. Might have him de-knighted too.

Called one's architect to enquire about having the Tower of London extended, just in case. Queen Victoria always said it were better to have too much dungeon space than not enough.

- ## MONDAY 18TH JULY, 2011
'Tell one why one don't like Mondays.'

Hate Mondays. Henry I introduced them in 1101 to delay Tuesdays (he had a quite irrational fear of them – refused to reign on a Tuesday, apparently) and successive monarchs have considered abolishing them but the timing has never seemed quite right. Almost abolished them last year but Edward's birthday fell on a Monday and one didn't have the heart to make him wait a full twenty four months before getting a year older.

Woke to news that Mr Cameron was in South
Africa. Checked to see if one had exiled
him while under the influence last night but
apparently he's on a 'trade mission'. Very
seriously considering a trade mission of one's
own to trade Mr Cameron for a case of South
African wine. The DoE suspects it's actually
for a photocall with Mr Mandela. It never
ceases to amaze one that whenever a politician
of any country is facing trouble at home they
immediately assume that one photo with
Mandela will make everything all right. Sent him
a quick text ordering him back here immediately
to address the Commons on the phone hacking
scandal.

One's press secretary accidently re-faxed
Sir Paul Stephenson's resignation letter to
Scotland Yard; it was picked up by Assistant
Commissioner Yates who assumed it was for him
and immediately did the decent thing. Oh well.
There's plenty more fish in the sea, or plenty
more coppers at the yard, as it were.

The Duchess of Cornwall called to confirm that she hadn't resigned.

- TUESDAY 19TH JULY, 2011
'The DoE's just checking Mr Murdoch's voicemails in case there's anything urgent while he's at the Commons.'

Have cleared one's diary for the afternoon to watch Mr Murdoch's Commons Select Committee performance on TV. The DoE has gone in person, disguised as a policeman. He's taken Princess Anne's phone book with him, which he's hoping to sell for fifty quid. Mr Murdoch texted to ask if he could 'pop round' once he'd finished. Perhaps that was meant for Mr Cameron.

The show got under way about 2.30 p.m. It was like watching a particularly awkward episode of *Jeremy Kyle*. Wonderful TV though. Have texted the BBC Director General to suggest they do this every afternoon – it beats *Deal or No Deal* hands down. And if Tom Watson MP had a beard he'd look just like Noel Edmonds. The DoE texted to say he had checked Mr Murdoch's voicemails just in case there was anything urgent while he was at the Commons, which was nice of him. He's considerate like that.

The proceedings were halted when a member of the public covered Mr Murdoch in shaving foam. One hopes it wasn't the DoE. Popped off to get a cup of tea and came back to find the BBC showing an interview with Mick Hucknall from Simply Red. Watched for about half an hour before realising it was Rebekah Brooks giving evidence at the Commons. Was just about to text in and request he sung 'Stars'.

Went out for a walk with the corgis to find approximately five thousand people in one's garden. Remembered that one had planned a garden party, did some smiling and nodding and headed to the gin tent for a well deserved libation and, as it turned out, a discussion with a Mrs Edna Smith from Brixton about her bin collection. Assured her that it was her Queen's first priority and texted Mr Clegg to instruct him to get round there and sort it out.

8 p.m.: Accidently overdosed on gin and had to get a helicopter from the gin tent to the Palace terrace.

- **WEDNESDAY 20TH JULY, 2011**

'Mr Jobs, there is no such thing as "American English". There is English and there are mistakes.'

Woke rather late, thanks to gin-induced coma, the blame for which one is laying entirely at the door of Mrs Smith from Brixton (along with her bin, presumably). Mr Clegg texted to say her bin had been emptied. One likes to help. Thankfully one was only reigning in the Solomon Islands until 11 a.m., and they never usually notice if one's late, so had a quick bacon sandwich for security reasons.

Installed the new Apple operating system on one's MacBook Pro and realised Mr Jobs still hadn't fixed the 'American English' glitch. Text him to remind him that there is no such thing as 'American English'. There is English and there are mistakes. Waiting for a reply.

About to settle down for supper when Mr Clegg called again. In a bit of a state. Apparently his subscription to *My Little Pony Collector Magazine* is due for renewal and he's concerned that doing so may be construed as inappropriate contact with the media. Assured him that it was fine and he rang off relatively happy.

• Thursday 21st July, 2011

'Chancellor Merkel and President Sarkozy on a Skype call. Having a whip-round for Greece. One's popped in a tenner but one expects some change.'

Up at the crack of dawn by mistake. Took the opportunity to take the corgis out for a walk along the Mall and popped in on Clarence House for a cup of tea. Camilla was halfway through the hoovering but said she 'needed an excuse for a fag' so didn't mind taking a break. Apparently she always does the hoovering on a Thursday morning, mainly to avoid having to speak to Mrs 'value bunting' Middleton who always calls for a 'mothers' gossip'.

Back to the Palace for lunch and a Skype call with Chancellor Merkel and President Sarkozy. They're having a whip-round for Greece. One popped in a tenner but took five pounds change. If things get really bad they can always reinstate the monarchy.

Andrew came round to discuss his role as UK Special Representative for International Trade. Says, after ten years in the job, he feels he really ought to step down and concentrate, as Duke of York, on marching his 10,000 men up to the top of the hill and marching them down again. Quite right too. Texted Mr Cameron to tell him the bad news. He said the Government was naturally devastated but they'd try and cope as best they could.

- **Friday 22nd July, 2011**
'I name this day Friday.'

Friday at last. Reigning all week. Final
preparations for Zara's wedding to Mike Tindall
are under way. Poor thing wanted to sell the
rights to *Hello!* magazine but one's had to put
one's foot down and say no on account of this
being a Royal Wedding and not, as the DoE
would say, a 'piss-up at the Rugby Club'.

Eight days to go. Anne is frantic with worry. She
briefly considered a new hairstyle in celebration
but has instead opted for a new hat. One's had
Mr Clegg sent up to make sure that the Royal
Mile is swept properly (after his success with
Mrs Smith's Brixton bin collection, one's got
him increasingly focused on rubbish).

Finally some sunshine. July was starting to
feel like midwinter. One's motivational call to
the Archbishop of Canterbury last night must
have done the trick. Headed over to Windsor

a day early for some well deserved rest and relaxation.

Very sad to hear of the death of Lucian Freud. He made one look rather fetching. And the DoE and I were absolutely devastated to learn of the truly dreadful events in Norway. Sent a message of support and condolence to King Harald expressing one's deepest sympathies.

- SATURDAY 23RD JULY, 2011

'Someone get one a pot of tea.'

Quiet day at Windsor, starting with a couple of poached eggs and a bowl of Coco Pops. Zara popped over with Mr Tindall to run through the final wedding preparations. Apparently the entire England Rugby Team are coming.

- SUNDAY 24TH JULY, 2011

'One likes to get one's shopping at the Royal Farm shop. Every little helps.'

Glorious sunshine today. Got up early and headed out for a long walk with the corgis and a catch up with one's estate manager. Popped over to the Royal Windsor Farm Shop on the way back to the Castle for a jar of honey and a loaf of bread. That place has proved to be something of a goldmine, stocking produce from the Royal Farms. The DoE is thinking of opening a chain of them throughout the UK.

Back to the Castle for the afternoon. Mrs 'there's really no need to call me Mrs Middleton' Middleton has sent over a Swiss roll that she'd baked, so the DoE and I tucked into that with a cup of tea.

- MONDAY 25TH JULY, 2011
'Someone get one a gin and ginger ale. No ginger ale.'

Back to London to finish up on some Head of State business before heading off to Scotland at the end of the week for Zara's wedding and then on to Balmoral for one's summer holiday. Did a quick investiture in the afternoon for various worthwhiles and settled down in the evening to watch *EastEnders* on iPlayer with a large gin and ginger ale with no ginger ale.

- **TUESDAY 26TH JULY, 2011**

'Don't even think about blaming the Royal Wedding, Cameron. You're on thin ice, moonbeam.'

Mr Cameron called first thing. One had only just polished off a bacon and cheese butty. Wanted to 'forewarn' one that the economic growth figures aren't looking too rosy. Tried to blame the Royal Wedding but one set him straight. One does wonder what part of 'grow the economy' he didn't understand when moving into Downing Street. He assured me that Mr Osborne was up to the job and said that his newly acquired GCSE in Maths would help.

Lewis Hamilton called to complain that
the National Anthem isn't long enough and
wondered if one might change it. Told him to
concentrate on driving a car and that his Queen
would concentrate on driving a nation. The
National Anthem is not changing.

- **WEDNESDAY 27TH JULY, 2011**
*'Yes, very interesting Lord Coe. Is that all? One has
a few other things to be getting on with.'*

Lord Coe called first thing to remind one that
we are only a year from the London Olympics.
One expressed one's disappointment that like
almost everyone else in the United Kingdom,
one didn't manage to get tickets in the ballot. He
apologised again but said that he had managed to
get Edward tickets to the men's volleyball. He'll
be so excited.

Mr Clegg called to ask if one would be requiring
use of his Downing Street paddling pool and
sandpit for the Olympics, or his trampoline.

Gave him Lord Coe's number but said that one suspected that they would probably manage fine without.

Not really looking forward to the Olympics. It seems that they'll be a pain in the arse for Londoners and of little interest to anyone outside. And quite frankly a bit of a distraction from one's Diamond Jubilee. Mr Cameron said the opening ceremony would be an excellent opportunity to showcase Britain as a 'progressive, modern democracy finding its place in a twenty-first-century world'. Which presumably means David Beckham dressed like a girl and kicking a football from the top of a London bus.

Just about to knock off for the day when Mr Miliband called to ask if he could put his nose job through on expenses. No.

• THURSDAY 28TH JULY, 2011
'Approximately 87% of the Civil List is transferred directly into British Gas' bank account.'

Awoke to the truly wonderful news that British
Gas has made another huge profit. Could hardly
contain one's delight. No doubt they'll be
immediately cutting fuel bills.

• FRIDAY 29TH JULY, 2011
'No sign of Pippa Middleton. Awkward'

Arrived at the Palace of Holyroodhouse, one's
official residence in Scotland, for Zara's wedding
tomorrow. If Mr Tindall hasn't had his nose done,
the whole thing is off. The rest of the family have
also arrived. Anne is beside herself with excitement.
She went out for a long walk with Camilla, who after
William's wedding in April is something of a pro at
these things. Unfortunately they got lost in the back
streets of Edinburgh and had to get a taxi back.

Zara has arranged a party aboard the Royal Yacht
Britannia for this evening. Harry has invited Pippa
Middleton's bottom, but he's not sure if it's coming.
The DoE and I decided to give it a miss. One loved
that ship and doesn't really want to see it moored

as a tourist attraction. Stayed in at Holyroodhouse and toasted the bride and groom with a bottle of Scottish whisky and a box of shortbread.

Harry came home late and managed to wake everyone up by knocking a seventeenth-century vase off of a sideboard. Apparently Pippa Middleton's bottom didn't show.

- ### SATURDAY 30TH JULY, 2011
'Beatrice has revealed her wedding hat. Hushed silence.'

Wedding day. Second Royal Wedding of the year, although this one is a little less high-profile. The DoE made a round of bacon sandwiches for the assembled guests. Anne had a bowl of Coco Pops as she's worried about getting into her outfit.

Beatrice says she is leaving it to the last minute to reveal her hat. One suspects that it'll be on eBay by tonight. The DoE popped out to get a giant pretzel and Superglued it to an upturned paper plate, which he said she could always wear if she fancied continuing the previous wedding hat theme. Awkward.

The DoE emerged about midday in a New Zealand All Blacks Rugby strip. Told him he couldn't wear that to the wedding, no matter how funny he'd find the look on the Tindalls' faces.

Slight interruption in the proceedings to bollock Revenue and Customs for terrible customer service. Reminded them that one put the HM into HMRC and one could take it out again.

Edward was glued to the new series of *ThunderCats*. Had to switch the TV off before he finally went upstairs to get dressed. How the Countess of Wessex puts up with all those cartoons, one will never know.

We all jumped in the cars about 2.45 p.m. and headed down to Canongate Kirk on the Royal Mile for the service. Mr Tindall had been planning on wearing a kilt but the DoE managed to talk him out of it on account of the infamous draught in the nave. If there's one thing one could really do without looking at, it's Mr Tindall's nether regions.

It all went very well. One felt sorry for the people sitting behind the Duchess of Cambridge. One can't imagine they managed to see a great deal over her hat. Still, at least it wasn't quite the embarrassment that Beatrice managed at William's wedding. The DoE thinks it'll make at least two hundred quid on eBay though.

Back to the Palace of Holyroodhouse for a few mini-burger and cocktail sausage canapés before changing for this evening's Rugby-themed fancy dress party. Camilla and Charles came as a goalpost, each painted white and attached with a horizontal pole. The DoE said it was the most time they had ever spent together. All seemed to go OK though, until Camilla popped out for a

cigarette and in doing so dragged Charles away
from a plate of smoked salmon.

- **SUNDAY 31ST JULY, 2011**
*'OK Balmoral. Backs to the walls. The Queen is
coming.'*

Morning after the night before. Absolute empire
of a hangover. Had completely forgotten that one
was at Holyroodhouse and awoke wondering
why someone had changed all the furniture.

The DoE was up early and cooking everyone
a full Scottish breakfast of eggs, bacon and
sausage, black pudding, haggis and tattie scones,
fried tomatoes, baked beans, white pudding,
fruit pudding and oatcakes. Washed down with
a traditional wee dram of Scottish whisky to
combat the hangover. Camilla always says the
best way to avoid a hangover is not to go to bed
and to carry on drinking until breakfast, which
seemed to have done the trick as she was perky
as anything.

Zara and Mr Tindall came down in time for the
DoE's special poached eggs. They're delaying
their honeymoon due to sporting commitments.
Anne looked every inch the proud mother, and
one has to hand it to Mr Tindall, he can down a
pint of bitter like nobody's business.

Went out for a family walk with the corgis to get
some fresh air and work off the breakfast. Willow
the corgi saw a rabbit and chased it down a hole,
getting stuck in the process. It took about six
of us and a piece of rope to get her out again.
Luckily Camilla went down the other end and
managed to push Willow back through.

Back to Holyroodhouse for supper and then
into the helicopter and off to Balmoral for one's
annual summer break with the DoE.

AUGUST AND SEPTEMBER

Summer at Balmoral

- Monday 1st August, 2011

'Dear American Congress, any more sodding around and one is having you and your "independence" dissolved. Your ever gracious Queen, EIIR.'

First morning of the year at Balmoral Castle, one's summer estate in Royal Deeside, Aberdeenshire. It's been in the family since 1852, when Queen Victoria and Prince Albert bought it as a little Scottish hideaway. Of course, the original house was far too small and was demolished to make way for the current castle, completed during 1856 with a bit of architectural input from Prince Albert. It's one's favourite retreat. About 50,000 acres of grouse moors, farmland and forests, as well as herds of deer, Highland cattle and ponies: bliss. Charles and Camilla have a little getaway just down the road – Birkhall.

The DoE and I were up early for an inspection of the house. One's household come up the week before and have a bit of a dust and hoover. There's not an inch of wall not covered by something the DoE has killed.

Had a very difficult Skype call with the American Congress after lunch to tell them to stop acting like a bunch of imbeciles and sort out their debt problem before one had them and their independence dissolved, or worse, sent Mr Blair over. They took it quite well (apparently – one had hung up by then).

Out for a long walk with the corgis in the afternoon. They do love it up here. Although Monty managed to clamp his jaws around the arse of a deer about ten times his size and was carried off into the distance. He'll probably be back for his supper.

Got back to the Castle for mid-afternoon and in time for *Come Dine with Me*. Had some Scottish gin opened and spent the evening reading Queen Victoria's diaries – not the published edition but the originals. Heavy editing clearly required for published Royal Diaries. Note to self.

• TUESDAY 2ND AUGUST, 2011
'How about never, Mr Clegg? Does never work for you?'

Mr Clegg called first thing to check what date he was required at Balmoral. After a bit of discussion we agreed that never was looking pretty good for us both. He said he'd pencil it in and look forward to it. The DoE says we ought to let him come as he could do with someone to hold his gun on shoots. Although given what he's managed to sod up in Government, one's not sure that letting him loose with a dangerous weapon is such a good idea.

Spent the afternoon catching up on Scottish business. Mr Salmond, the First Minister, had sent over a pile of briefing notes. He's determined to push through an independence referendum but says one can stay as Queen. How kind. The DoE and I had a quick referendum and decided unanimously that Mr Salmond is a moron.

One had warned Mr Blair that devolution would lead to calls for independence but, typically, he didn't listen. Still, one has every confidence that when push comes to shove one's people in Scotland won't want to sever the union.

Had a few friends round in the evening for a ceilidh. It was all going wonderfully until the DoE had a slight kilt malfunction and the Countess of Rosebery fainted. The party never really got going again afterwards so we retired a bit earlier than expected.

• **WEDNESDAY 3RD AUGUST, 2011**
'No Mr Cameron, one doesn't think that's a wonderful way of keeping the media informed.'

Mr Cameron called first thing to give one an update on the phone hacking enquiry. He said Lord Justice Leveson was making a start and that the media were being kept informed of progress via voicemails left on the answerphones of various MPs. One asked if that was perhaps in itself something to investigate and he said now that he came to think of it, it probably was and he'd get the Met onto it right away.

• THURSDAY 4TH AUGUST, 2011
'Considering doing Come Dine with One.*'*

The Earl and Countess of Stair popped over mid-morning for tea and Custard Creams and a catch-up on the local gossip. Apparently there was a rather embarrassing episode at the post office last week. They didn't go into details but the DoE thought that might be why Balmoral hasn't had any post so far this month.

Went for a walk with the Countess and the corgis and we discussed doing our own show: *Come Dine with One*. She said she'd see if she could get a few more interested. Of course, we'd have to update the rules to allow for chefs, cooks, kitchen staff, maids and butlers etc.

- ### Friday 5th August, 2011
'If anyone sees Camilla, pop her in a taxi to Birkhall.'

Edinburgh Fringe Festival Party at the Royal Household this evening. The DoE is headlining, naturally, and Camilla is supporting with her first ever stand-up routine. All very exciting. We've had the cinema set up with a stage and a few locals are coming over for Pimm's on the terrace beforehand.

9 p.m.: Camilla was absolutely hilarious, although said afterwards that she didn't get a chance to get into her routine and had simply been recounting her afternoon. The DoE stole the show though with his political impressions, including changing into short trousers for the Mr Clegg routine. Might send the Cabinet a DVD of it.

Much whisky followed and we headed to bed around 1 a.m. Not sure what happened to Camilla. She popped out, determined to perform her proper routine to a herd of deer, and didn't return. The DoE thought perhaps she'd wandered back to Birkhall.

- ● SATURDAY 6TH AUGUST, 2011
'One does wish Princess Michael of Kent wouldn't do that at the table.'

The rest of the Royal Family arrive today: the Prince of Wales and the Duchess of Cornwall are already here (if we can find Camilla, that is); William and Catherine, the Duke and Duchess of Cambridge (fresh from Wales – William's flying in); Prince Harry (fresh from Pippa Middleton); Andrew, the Duke of York with Princess Beatrice and Princess Eugenie; Edward and Sophie, the Earl and Countess of Wessex and their children Viscount Severn and Lady Louise; Anne, the Princess Royal, and Vice Admiral Sir Timothy Laurence with Peter and Autumn Phillips and Zara and Mike Tindall; the Duke and Duchess of Gloucester; the Duke and Duchess of Kent; Prince and Princess Michael of Kent; and Princess Alexandra, the Honourable Lady Ogilvy. We're going for a BBQ and picnic.

The DoE and Charles loaded up the Range
Rovers first thing and went ahead to set up.
The DoE has as usual brought enough meat to
feed an army, let alone a Royal Family. The local
butcher came over first thing, selling eight legs
of venison for £50, but the DoE said it was too
dear (or two deer, one wasn't sure).

We had a light breakfast of poached eggs and
muffins with black pudding, so as not to spoil
lunch, and set off to join Charles and the DoE
about 11 a.m. Walked via Birkhall to see if we
could locate Camilla and sure enough found her
in the garden digging a swimming pool. She said
she'd just get changed into something a little
more comfortable and would catch us up.

We finally arrived at the picnic site about 2 p.m.
Luckily the DoE had lit a fire so big that we were
guided in by smoke signals for the last few miles.
Got there to find the DoE covered in soot and
standing over an enormous BBQ. Charles had
set out the picnic and we all settled down to a

generous amount of gin and Dubonnet with ice and a slice. Camilla arrived a few minutes afterwards and was slightly disappointed to see the BBQ as she'd assumed the smoke meant we'd started on the cigars already.

Lovely afternoon until Willow the corgi stole a sausage from Princess Michael's plate and she used a word Mr Tindall has never before heard off of the Rugby field. Still, she managed to prise it from Willow's jaws, dipped it in a glass of gin to wash it off and popped it back in her bun, so all was well that ended well.

Charles accidentally set fire to Camilla just as we were leaving but she jumped in the lake so no harm done. We traipsed back to Balmoral, taking the long route, and all popped in on one's estate manager for a cup of tea and a slice of apple cake. All but Camilla, who decided to swim home. We did try and tell her it's a lake and therefore land-locked but she said she was sure she'd seen a tributary somewhere.

Had to pop off to a local phone box and make a couple of 'head of state' calls – one can never get a signal on one's iPhone in the Highlands. Had America's credit rating downgraded to AA (Americans Anonymous) and Italy's to C-. Had Greece put on detention.

Spent the evening playing 'If I Were Queen', where everyone takes it in turns to give a Queen's speech of things they'd like to legislate for in the next parliament. These ideas are all collated by one's private secretary and sent to Mr Cameron for consideration.

Ended the day in a lake of gin.

• SUNDAY 7TH AUGUST, 2011
'You'll have to throw it back, Camilla. It'll never start.'

Up at the crack of dawn. The Duke of Kent was making one of his 'special breakfasts' of fried bacon, baked beans, fried bread, black pudding, bubble and squeak, corned beef hash, eggs (fried, poached and scrambled), English muffins, French toast, fruit pudding, hash browns, kidneys (grilled and fried), kippers, fried mushrooms, oatcakes, pancakes, sautéed potatoes, potato bread, sausages, laverbread, toast, fried, grilled and tinned tomatoes, potato waffles and white pudding. Nice for the DoE to have a day off breakfast duty.

We finished breakfast about 3 p.m. (the Duke of Kent insists that everyone clear their plates) and all went out for the annual fishing trip. The DoE caught a 4lb trout and we were just about to leave when Camilla said she'd landed a 'big un' and we all stood round to watch her reel in a Ford Escort.

We headed back to the house (minus the Escort, which Camilla reluctantly agreed to throw back in) for a trout supper and Queen Karaoke. Notable performances from Princess Michael ('I Want it All'), Camilla ('I Want to Break Free'), Edward ('Bicycle Race'), Andrew ('Fat Bottomed Girls') and the DoE ('Don't Stop Me Now').

- ### MONDAY 8TH AUGUST, 2011
'OK kiddies, party over.'

Absolutely appalled at the violence in London this evening. Have sent a message of support to one's people to keep calm and carry on. We shall prevail. Sent Boris Johnson to Tottenham with a fire extinguisher. Ed Miliband called to say he was cutting short his holiday, which one was sure would be of endless comfort to one's people if any of them actually knew who he was. Sent a message to Cameron and Osborne telling them to pack up their buckets and spades and get on a plane.

- ### SUNDAY 21ST AUGUST, 2011
'No, Mr Clegg, people born in Libya are not "librarians"'

Awake early and just about to go out with the corgis when Colonel Gaddafi text ('bollocks'), which was quite a shock as one was quite sure he'd been deposed months ago. Mr Cameron called to say that rebels had stormed Tripoli

Contents of the Royal Handbag

1. Miniature gin
2. Reading glasses
3. Packet of Soft Mints
4. Royal iPhone
5. Crown-embossed tissues
6. Remote control for nuclear weapons
7. Hatpin

(which Camilla thought was a Libyan value food shop) and that it wasn't looking good for the Colonel. Well, he's not pitching his tent on one's lawn, that's a sure thing. One has only just managed to persuade Andrew to move back into the palace, female body guards and all.

Mr Clegg called to ask what the problem was with 'Libra' and wondered if one thought the problem may spread to other star signs. One unfortunately was unable to answer, mainly due to having hung up and taken the corgis out for a spin in the Range Rover.

Spent the day on the moors and returned about 6ish for a Libyan gin cocktail and toasted a brighter future for North Africa.

• THURSDAY 1ST SEPTEMBER, 2011
'Oh Christ. Mr Cameron's in a kilt!'

All peace shattered. The Camerons are coming for their annual Scottish visit. It's a bizarre ritual: prime ministers and their spouses don't like visiting Balmoral, the DoE and I don't like prime ministers and their spouses visiting Balmoral, but somehow no one likes to suggest that we give it a miss.

Mr and Mrs Cameron arrived about midday by helicopter. Oh good God, he's wearing a kilt. Those legs should never, ever see the light of day. And by the look of them they never have.

The DoE had to pop on a pair of sunglasses; they were positively reflective. And those knees. One hasn't seen knees that bad since Cherie Blair. The DoE said he'd seen better legs on IKEA furniture, but thankfully Mr Cameron didn't hear him over the helicopter noise.

Showed them to their rooms and gave them the rest of the time to settle in. They took an impromptu walk around the grounds about 5ish and the DoE nearly shot them by mistake. Not sure Mrs Cameron will ever recover from the shock. The bullet missed her by a good few inches so not sure what she's worrying about.

Quiet supper of salmon. Mr Cameron told us all about the happenings in London. Apparently Mr Clegg has been drawing on the walls again, but Mr Cameron's hoping it's just a phase he's going through. He's apparently still very unsettled by the Downing Street cat. That said, Mrs Cameron reported that he had caught some rats, which is more than can be said for the cat, by all accounts.

We've had to leave Willow with Camilla at Birkhall after the Sandringham episode. Mr Cameron has apparently only been able to rest his full weight on his behind in the last month or so and didn't want to go through that again. He said the TCP the DoE gave him helped, although it apparently stung 'like hell' and smelled a bit like vinegar. The DoE said he couldn't imagine why.

● FRIDAY 2ND SEPTEMBER, 2011
'Willow the corgi has had her jaws around Cameron's arse. Again. Awkward.'

Mr and Mrs Cameron spent the day walking in the Highlands. The DoE gave them a map so they could avoid Birkhall and Willow but they took a wrong turn and she took the arse out of his trousers. Mrs Cameron said she'd never seen the Prime Minister run so fast. Willow can smell a prime minister at 400 yards and the poor chap didn't stand much of a chance. They opted for supper in their room and Mr Cameron spent the evening crouching in a bath of salt water.

• Saturday 3rd September, 2011
'Braemar Gathering. Mr Cameron says he'd have brought Mr Clegg if he'd known there was a children's sack race.'

Off to the Braemar Gathering, or the Scottish Highland Games, with Mr and Mrs Cameron today. One has managed to talk him out of wearing a kilt on account of the international PR disaster that would be sure to ensue.

The Braemar Gathering is one of one's favourite events of the year: Highland dancing, piping, tossing the caber, putting the stone, throwing the hammer, sprinting, relay race and hill race, long leap, tug of war and the children's sack race being the highlights of the programme.

Mr Cameron seemed to quite enjoy it after some initial reservations. He said that the tug of war had reminded him of last year's coalition negotiations and that if he had known there would be a children's sack race he would have brought Mr Clegg along to compete. The DoE said if there were any repeat of that kind of political indecision he'd be taking the long leap to Whitehall and throwing the hammer to get them all sprinting. Mr Cameron said he got the gist and would bear it in mind if a hung parliament were ever returned again.

We stayed to watch Camilla win the putting the stone competition, and headed home about 6 p.m. Edward stayed behind to have a go at tossing the caber.

- ## SUNDAY 4TH SEPTEMBER, 2011
'Popped the Camerons in their car and waved good riddance for another year.'

Up early for a farewell breakfast for the Prime Minister and Mrs Cameron. The DoE had knocked up a round of bacon and egg sandwiches and Camilla had baked some scones and popped them in a doggy bag for the journey. Mr Cameron said that the trip hadn't been anywhere as near as bad as he'd expected, which the DoE and I took as a compliment. The DoE assured him that it gets worse the longer he is in Government as a kind of constitutional check and balance to discourage long-serving prime ministers.

Waved them off mid-morning and had their room disinfected.

Spent the afternoon at Birkhall with Camilla and collected Willow. She still had the material from Mr Cameron's trousers in her mouth (Willow, that is, not Camilla). Camilla had brought the stone from the Braemar Gathering home with her and was chiselling it into a water feature.

Back to Balmoral for a quiet evening with the DoE and an almost unconstitutional amount of gin.

• MONDAY 5TH SEPTEMBER, 2011
'If one took a holiday . . . Took some time to celebrate . . .'

Decided to give oneself the rest of the month off writing diary. And ruling Ireland.

Agenda: Audience with the PM

1. *Replacement Royal Yacht*
2. *The Deputy PM*
3. *Carpet cleaning bill from his stay at Balmoral*
4. *The Deputy PM*
5. *Can we sell France?*

OCTOBER

Back to Work

- **Monday 3rd October, 2011**
'Here comes the reign again.'

Last day at Balmoral for another year. The DoE and I have had the last week to ourselves for a spot of walking and fishing and reflecting on the past year. Two Royal Weddings, a phone hacking crisis, a State Visit to Ireland and a State Visit by President and Mrs Obama. One really needed the break this year.

Mr Cameron called to say how much he and the Cabinet were looking forward to having one back in London, which was presumably a lie. The DoE popped over to Edinburgh mid-afternoon to commandeer the Royal Yacht *Britannia* but apparently her engines have been removed since the decommissioning. Shame. One was quite looking forward to seeing Mr Cameron's face as one sailed up the Thames.

Packed up the corgis and hopped into the helicopter for the flight back to Buckingham Palace.

• TUESDAY 4TH OCTOBER, 2011
'OK London, heads up. Your Queen has returned.'

Let it reign. One is back in London and taking personal charge. Had Mr Cameron round for an update. Very disappointed that he hasn't managed to show any meaningful economic growth over the summer. He put it down to leaving Mr Clegg in charge for a couple of weeks while he and Mrs Cameron had a short break in the Med. Told him that if he didn't start making some serious progress, one would have his guts for constitutional garters. He said he was just thrilled to have personal guidance once again. It is hard on one's politicians when one retreats to Scotland for the summer.

Mr Salmond called to say how much he'd enjoyed having his monarch in the country for a couple of months and how he hoped one would visit again soon. The DoE picked up the other line and told him to 'sod off' before one had a chance to respond.

Mr Clegg sent over a selection of crayon drawings he'd done over the summer. He'd left a space for Edward to colour in the grass and the sun, which one thought was awfully considerate of him.

• Wednesday 5th October, 2011
'Let's not do it, Mr Cameron. We don't enjoy each other's company that much.'

Up early to reacquaint the corgis with the Buckingham Palace Gardens. Popped into the Royal Mews on the way back to check on the horses and came back via the gift shop where one picked up a brief history of monarchy for Charles. Might pop it in his Christmas stocking. Spent the day catching up on State Papers. Told Mr Cameron not to bother coming over for his weekly audience as one had seen him on Monday.

Camilla popped over from Clarence House in the afternoon. Apparently the Harry and Pippa Middleton thing isn't going well. She thinks the poor girl is getting a bit tired of wearing that bridesmaid's dress every day but apparently Harry simply won't accept that her bottom looks as good in anything else.

William called in the afternoon to say that Catherine has finished decorating the Welsh cottage over the summer and that Mrs Middleton had sent over a lorryload of furniture that she'd got at a knocked-down price from the Habitat closure sale. She'd apparently also sent over a job lot of bunting, which she thought might come in handy for one's Diamond Jubilee next year. Awkward.

8 p.m.: The DoE and I settled down to an evening of London gin and fish and chips in front of the TV.

• Thursday 6th October, 2011

'Wondering how much one would get for Lord Coe on Cash in the Attic.*'*

Came back from an early morning walk with the corgis to find Lord Coe in one's sitting room. He'd come over to give one an update on Olympic progress while one was in Scotland. One smiled and nodded and tried awfully hard to look interested in his little sporting event. He said one would be 'a main attraction' at the opening ceremony. One does wish he wouldn't describe one as if one were a fairground ride. Popped him back on his skateboard and wished him well with the final preparations and settled down to *Cash in the Attic*. One really must see what's in the attic at Buckingham Palace if one ever gets a quiet weekend. Apparently hardly anyone has been up there since Queen Victoria.

The Countess of Wessex took Edward on a visit to London Zoo in the afternoon. He came back with a cuddly penguin toy, from which he was inseparable for the rest of the evening.

9 p.m.: Charles and Camilla came over for drinks.

Bonfire Night and Christmas Preparations

- TUESDAY 1ST NOVEMBER, 2011

*'Staines shall not be changing its name to
"Staines-on-Thames". Not last year, not this year,
not ever.'*

Absolutely pissing with rain and freezing cold.
Sent the DoE out with a Barbour and the corgis
and stayed in by the fire. (Seriously considering
reigning in person in Australia during the winter
months. Texted Ms Gillard. She will be thrilled.)
He came back after about two hours minus Monty,
who apparently tried to shelter from the rain in a
badger sett and got stuck. Camilla went out with
a shovel, a packet of sausages and a length of rope
to try and retrieve the poor dog. Came back mid-
afternoon with Monty and about seven badgers.

Had a memo from the Leader of the Council in
Staines about the renaming again. Wants to call it
'Staines-on-Thames' and wondered if one would
intervene and push it through. One word: no.

2 p.m.: Spent the afternoon in front of the fire burning Government legislation and drinking sweet sherry.

• WEDNESDAY 2ND NOVEMBER, 2011
'Of course, the British have been testing weapons in France for hundreds of years.'

Mr Sarkozy on the phone first thing. Having signed a treaty with France last year paving the way for greater military cooperation and testing of nuclear weapons, he wondered if one now wanted use of his white flag factory. One politely declined, even if it is a key element of his military capability.

Called Mr Cameron to find out how the weapons tests with France were going. He assured one that these dangerous tests will be confined to a specific area, known as 'France'. Of course, the British have been testing weapons in France for hundreds of years.

*Playlist for iPod for carriage journey
to State Opening of Parliament*

1. Queen – 'Killer Queen'
2. Dolly Parton – 'Baby I'm
   Burning'
3. Rod Stewart – 'Handbags and
   Gladrags'
4. Abba – 'Take a Chance on Me'

5. Guns n' Roses – 'November Rain'
6. Cher – 'If I Could Turn Back
   Time'
7. Metallica – 'For Whom the Bell
   Tolls'
8. Lady Gaga – 'Bad Romance'
9. Johnny Cash – 'Ring of Fire'

- **THURSDAY 3RD NOVEMBER, 2011**

' "Sorry"? Mr Cameron? You're "Sorry"?'

Cleared one's diary and had the PM over to run one through why we remain in Europe. He said he was sorry, felt bullied by the Germans, didn't want to be left out, trying to please Mr Clegg etc. Told him not to worry: it's only 1,000 years of independence and global supremacy he's putting at risk, after all. Told him that unless he wanted to be a Euro MP inside six weeks he'd better pull his socks up.

- **FRIDAY 4TH NOVEMBER, 2011**

'DoE is busy making effigies of the entire House of Commons to burn on Guy Fawkes night.'

Took the day off to prepare for tomorrow's Royal Bonfire Party. DoE spent the entire day making effigies of the entire House of Commons to burn. Had a few sweet sherries to warm the cockles before bed.

• SATURDAY 5TH NOVEMBER, 2011
'Royal Bonfire Party. Andrew loves a whizz-bang.'

Never drinking again. Ever. Never mind parliament, the only thing one was dissolving this morning was a paracetamol. Nothing that a sausage sandwich didn't sort out.

Royal Bonfire Party this evening. Tucked into a jacket potato and a sausage while the DoE got under way with his bonfire of MP effigies and Edward amused himself by writing his name with a sparkler.

Clegg first on; strange blue tinge to the yellow flame. Cameron effigy was next on. Appeared to be melting rather than burning. Followed by the Ed Miliband effigy, which quite honestly never really got going. The Lord Sugar effigy was next and the DoE took great pleasure in shouting, 'You're fired!' as he chucked him on. Then came the Blair effigy. We all stood back as the DoE had dipped that one in petrol. Must admit, Mr

Campbell's memoirs burned nicely too. Final effigy of the night was Gordon Brown, defiantly refusing to burn among the embers of a dying fire.

Camilla had brought a box of fireworks over but accidentally dropped a fag on them, which made for an impressive but somewhat hazardous (and ultimately short-lived) bang. She said it was something she'd come to live with since marrying Charles.

Inside for a round of mulled wine. Andrew stayed up late roasting his nuts over the fire.

• MONDAY 14TH NOVEMBER, 2011
'Gin O'Clock.'

Final day in London before heading back to Sandringham for Christmas. A couple of weeks early this year; one wanted to get a good rest in before the Diamond Jubilee next year.

What a year 2011 has been. William and
Catherine getting married and then conquering
Canada and America; Zara and Mr Tindall
married; one's first visit to Ireland and the
historic Bono treaty; having the Obamas over
for President Obama's annual appraisal. To say
nothing of having to close a national newspaper.
And how Mr Cameron and Mr Clegg are still
together one may never know.

Going to do some Christmas shopping when
one gets to Sandringham. Might buy Charles a
small island in the Pacific or something so he
can get some ruling practice in. Edward's asked
for a Lego pirate ship. Harry has asked for Pippa
Middleton.

2012 is going to be a busy one: the Olympics, one's
Diamond Jubilee. One will be only the second
monarch ever to celebrate a Diamond Jubilee,
Queen Victoria being the first. At least one will
have the DoE by one's side. How Queen Victoria
must have wished Albert had been there to witness

hers. One's decided to have a little concert at
Buckingham Palace and a flotilla down the Thames.
And if Cameron doesn't get his act together one
might top it off with a general election.

2012

New Year, Valentine's Day and one's Diamond Jubilee

- Sᴜɴᴅᴀʏ 1ꜱᴛ Jᴀɴᴜᴀʀʏ 2012

Diamond Jubilee year. What a prospect. On 6th February one will have been Queen Regnant for sixty years. One was up a tree when the DoE broke the news. It's often said that one went up a Princess and came down a Queen. Elton John had a similar experience, one understands.

Made a note of one's 2012 resolutions:
1. ~~Give up gin~~
2. Buy a barge for Diamond Jubilee river pageant
3. Have France moved further away
4. Get Gary Barlow to organise a little concert at Buckingham Palace
5. Knight Brian May
6. Look into Making Dannii Minogue Australian PM (or Rolf Harris, whoever is available)
7. Wean Mr Cameron off the dummy (Mr Clegg)

8. Find a Leader of the Opposition who can talk in fully formed sentences
9. Hook up the Queen of Spain with Phillip Schofield

The DoE seems to be getting back to his old self, after giving us all a scare at Christmas. Not sure what one would do without the old chap, to be honest. All these years he's been there: two steps behind. Queen Victoria never got over the loss of Prince Albert. One was getting a bit reflective when the DoE appeared with a plate of sausages arranged in a '2012' shape. He always knows how to get one back on track.

Mr Cameron called to wish one a Happy New Year and said that one's Diamond Jubilee and the Olympics would make this a year to remember. One told him that if he didn't get the economy moving one would give him a general election to remember the year by. He said there was someone on the other line and sadly couldn't stop for a chat.

Sent breakfast up to Camilla but she apparently didn't make it to bed last night. We found her later in the afternoon up a tree – Charles had apparently popped her up there in the hope she'd come down a Queen.

- MONDAY 9TH JANUARY 2012 –
CATHERINE'S BIRTHDAY

Had everyone round to Sandringham to celebrate the Duchess of Cambridge's Birthday. It's the first birthday she's celebrated as a member of the Royal Family. She said she didn't want anything expensive, so one bought her France. Told her to play it down though, they've never been Queen fans since Marie Antoinette. Even Freddie Mercury struggled to sell records over there, apparently.

William and Catherine wanted to celebrate her birthday alone in the evening so we gathered for a birthday lunch instead. William popped down to Berkshire to collect Mr and Mrs Middleton in his

helicopter, which Mr Middleton said they very
much appreciated . . . although Mrs Middleton said
she would have preferred it if he hadn't winched
them aboard. Once an RAF search and rescue pilot,
always an RAF search and rescue pilot.

Mrs Middleton has developed a bizarre
habit of curtseying almost to the floor with a
breathless 'Your Royal Highness' every time she
sees Catherine since the wedding, which quite
frankly is awkward in the extreme. The DoE
calls her 'Queen Mother in waiting'.

We sat down to a turkey curry and Catherine
gave a little speech about how much she'd
enjoyed being Royal and how much everyone
had welcomed her. Mrs Middleton stood up
to give a speech afterwards, but sadly none of
us heard it, thanks in part to the DoE who had
taken everyone out for a post-lunch shoot.

Antony Worrall Thompson called in the
afternoon, asking to borrow a tenner. He's

been caught shoplifting from Tesco. The police apparently found a lump of cheese, a bottle of wine and an onion in his bag and gave him fifteen minutes to make a three-course meal from them.

Mr Cameron called in the evening to say he was giving the go-ahead for a high-speed rail link to Birmingham, as requested. BIRMINGHAM?! No, no, no, one said Balmoral! Who wants to get to Birmingham in a hurry, for Christ sake?! Apparently too late to change it now but he assures one that he'll have it extended to Balmoral 'ASAP'. Whatever.

- **Friday 13th January 2012**

Downgraded France's credit rating from AAA to AA. Poor chap was a little distraught but the DoE told him to look on the bright side: the AA would come in very handy if his car breaks down. Not sure if he saw the funny side, to be honest.

10pm: Popped France on eBay, on a strictly 'buyer collects' basis.

- SATURDAY 28TH JANUARY 2012

Decided to have a concert to celebrate one's Diamond Jubilee. Got Gary Barlow on the phone, as he seems to like organising these things. He said 'it would be an honour and a privilege' but was a bit worried it might put Elton John's nose out. One assured him that Elton John would be thrilled if he were asked to hand out the cheese straws backstage and to get on with organising it quick-smart. He said he'd pop round to Buckingham Palace and do a bit of measuring up.

4pm: Oh great, the Spice Girls are reforming for one's Diamond Jubilee. Well, that'll be worth sixty years of reigning for. The sodding Spice Girls. Text Gary Barlow and asked him what part of Led Zeppelin he didn't understand. He said it was nothing to do with him and that he wasn't even thinking about performers until he'd got the stage built. Assured him that one really, really, really does not want a 'zigazig ha'. What happened to Brian May for Christ's sake?!

If there's one thing that'll sod up one's Diamond
Jubilee it's Victoria bloody Beckham.

• **TUESDAY 31ST JANUARY** 2012
Out for an early morning walk with the corgis.
It is absolutely freezing in Norfolk. Popped in
on one's estate manager for an iced bun and
a catch up on the gossip before heading back
to the house for some motivational world
leadership.

Have decided to have a bit of a sort-out before
January is done. Started with stripping Fred
Goodwin of his knighthood. Frightful little
man has caused havoc in one's economy. Light
lunch of Shepherd's Pie before sending the
destroyer HMS Dauntless to the Falklands to
keep an eye on the Argentines. Also decided to
send William out there to take personal charge.
Andrew wanted to go too but was sadly stuck at
Sandringham, due in part to the DoE who had
locked him in his bedroom.

Sent a memo to everyone who has ever been knighted warning them that hell hath no fury like a Queen scorned, and nearly de-lorded Jeffrey Archer to prove the point but ran out of time.

• MONDAY 6TH FEBRUARY 2012 – ACCESSION DAY
Accession Day. Happy Diamond Jubilee to me, Happy Diamond Jubilee to me, Happy Diamond Jubilee my Majesty, Happy Diamond Jubilee to me! Yes, one is the first British monarch to celebrate a Diamond Jubilee since Queen Victoria. Sixty years in charge today.

Of course, it's always something of a double-edged sword, accession day, as it's also the anniversary of the death of one's beloved father, King George VI. One often wonders what he would have made of Britain today. He's probably rolling in his grave if he can see the muppets in Government. And it's a difficult day for Charles too, another year older and another year not King. Still, William and Harry have made him a surprise pretend Throne Room in the shed at Sandringham with a huge chair decorated in foil and a plastic crown, so that should cheer him up a bit.

Started the day with a visit to a primary school in Norfolk, which was actually like being in a shadow cabinet meeting, although quite frankly the quality of the colouring-in was better.

Back to Sandringham to prepare for this evening's Diamond Jubilee party. Mr Cameron called to congratulate one of reaching 'such a magnificent milestone' and to say that one was 'a source of great comfort and continuity to the nation and the world', or something like that. One couldn't really hear him to be honest, partly because one had popped him on hold and gone for a quick pedicure.

8pm: One's coming up so you'd better get this party started! Diamond Jubilee theme for this evening's Diamond Jubilee fancy dress party. Camilla misread the invitation as 'Jubilee Line

Party' and came dressed as a tube train, which was awkward. Although she did arrive late, which one thought was ironically appropriate. Had to point out to Edward that sequins are not an acceptable substitute for diamonds, and besides which, we have all seen that Shirley Bassey outfit before. He disappeared in a puff of powder and reappeared in a Freddie Mercury-style diamond jump suit.

Edward kicked off the karaoke with 'Diamonds are Forever', with Beatrice and Eugenie on backing vocals, followed by Charles with his version of 'Diamonds and Pearls' – he's such a Prince fan. William is away protecting the Falklands but Catherine and Andrew stole the show with a duet of Madonna's 'Material Girl' before Camilla stunned everyone into silence with a Marilyn Manson inspired heavy metal version of 'Diamonds Are a Girl's Best Friend'.

The DoE was about to get up for his go when Neil Diamond arrived. A-maz-ing. William had

apparently organised it. We all joined in for
'Cracklin' Rosie' before one took to the stage
for an encore of 'Killer Queen' with Brian May
on guitar, although since the Golden Jubilee he
insists on playing his solo from the roof.

No idea what happened to Camilla. She was
apparently last seen walking towards the potting
shed with Neil Diamond over her shoulder.
One does hope she doesn't disturb one's Busy
Lizzies.

• MONDAY 13TH FEBRUARY 2012

First day back at work after the Christmas break.
One thought Sandringham was cold enough but
London is absolutely sodding freezing. It took
the DoE all morning to thaw out Linnet the corgi
with a hairdryer. Apparently Camilla has been on
some kind of rotisserie machine since Saturday.

Pinky and Perky (Cameron and Clegg) popped up
on Skype to talk one through the progress they'd
failed to make while one had been away. All

the fault of the last Government/the Eurozone/
Greeks/French apparently, nothing they could
have done differently etc. Really, it's like
listening to a couple of naughty school children.
Popped them on report and wrote a note to their
mothers to say they'd be permanently excluded
from Government unless they bucked up their
ideas and settled down for The Jeremy Kyle
Show. Watched it for a full forty-five minutes
until realising one was watching live coverage of
the Leveson Enquiry. Awkward.

Has Gary Sodding Barlow actually moved in?
He's in Buckingham Palace more than his
Queen. Nipped into the Ball Room this afternoon
to pop a Led Zeppelin DVD on the cinema screen
and there he was, walking around with a
clipboard like some kind of cross between a
pop star and a food hygiene inspector. He said
plans for one's Diamond Jubilee Concert were
coming on nicely. Elton John and Cliff Richard
have apparently confirmed, which struck one
as deeply unimaginative. One wonders if Elton

John does anything else other than Royal births, marriages, deaths and jubilees these days. Still, one smiled and nodded and had him wheeled out into the forecourt.

Settled down in the evening to watch the second instalment of that Andrew Marr chap's documentary about one's sixty years on the throne. The DoE was close to taking out a restraining order on him by the end of last year. He's been following one around like a corgi, although not as well house-trained by all accounts. Still, nice to see Beatrice on TV without an embarrassingly inappropriate hat for a change.

11pm: Just dropped off to sleep when one's Private Secretary woke one up with news that Moody's credit agency had placed the UK's AAA credit rating on 'negative outlook'. The cheeky sods. Sent them a memo to remind them that one is not French and not to even think about downgrading one's rating. Sent a text to Chancellor Merkel to remind her that if her

Monopoly-money-currency meant one lost one's AAA credit rating, one would be sending a lot of big boats over to get it back. Sodding Europeans.

And what on earth is Gary Barlow STILL doing here? It's 1am and he's outside with a tape measure and a sketch pad. How much organising does one Diamond Jubilee concert need?

Tuesday 14th February – Valentine's Day

Nearly slept through one's alarm this morning, thanks to late night European-induced stress. Really, a Diamond Queen needs more sleep than this. The DoE popped in with a bacon sandwich cut into a heart shape for Valentine's Day – the old romantic – and Edward brought in the first enormous post bag of cards. Sent a quick message to the Commonwealth assuring them that no one loves them more than their Queen and had a quick read through one's Valentine's Day text messages:

- Text from the Pope: 'You are the Queen, I am the Pope, I know you don't fancy me but I still live in hope'. (One didn't reply)

- Text from Gary Barlow: 'Whatever I said, whatever I did I didn't mean it. I just want you back for good'. (One shall never forgive Lulu for relighting that man's fire)

- Text from Nick Clegg: 'Haven't forgotten your Valentine's card mum. Just finishing the colouring in!'. (One does wish he wouldn't call one 'mum')

- Text from the Queen of Spain: 'OMG just imagine waking up on Valentine's Day in the shadow of Phillip Schofield'. (She loves that man.)

- Text from Mr Cameron: 'Happy Valentine's Day your gracious majesty'. (That man is such a sycophant.)

Just settled down to the Racing Post when the President of Argentina emailed to say that Sean Penn thinks the Falklands should belong to Argentina. Who is Sean Penn? The DoE thought it was the name Mr Clegg gives to stationery. Decided to introduce legislation requiring him to be known as 'Sean Pencil' henceforth. The interfering little sod. Replied to the President of Argentina pointing out that The Queen thinks they should remain British and popped a couple of grand on the 2.15 at Kempton.

Charles and Camilla came over for dinner in the evening. Camilla rushed in very excited and thanked Charles for the beautiful bunch of flowers he'd sent her for Valentine's Day, which was a bit awkward as they were apparently not from him. Turns out they were from her gin supplier, so all's well that ends well.

Ended the day with a nightcap of gin martinis and Mini Cheddars and headed off to bed.

MONDAY 12TH MARCH 2012 –
COMMONWEALTH DAY
Arrived back at Buckingham Palace from Windsor almost unconstitutionally late. Thanks

in part to the annual 'Commonwealth Day Eve Disco' at the Castle. This year had a special rock theme and one was up until the early hours taking in the Guns 'n' Roses medley. Not entirely sure what happened to Camilla; she was last seen on a horse singing 'The Show Must Go On' and heading towards the Great Park.

Today is Commonwealth Day, an annual opportunity for the world to come together in loving homage to their undoubted and gracious Queen. The DoE knocked up a 'Commonwealth breakfast' (consisting of the national breakfasts of each member state) and one started proceedings with a Skype call to the various heads of government. Mohamed Nasheed of the Maldives wasn't there of course, having been ousted in a coup. The DoE says no one should ever be ousted 'and certainly not in a coupe'. One didn't say anything.

The Australians were up first. Poor old Julia Gillard has been having a bit of difficulty down there keeping control of things so it turned into a sort of counselling session-come-group therapy. One was about to get Dannii Minogue on the phone to form a new Government when the Canadian Prime Minister helpfully pointed out that there were 54 nations in the Commonwealth and that the other 53 were getting a little tired of 'listening to such self indulgent crap'. One doesn't like to comment, of course, but she was rather going on a bit.

Long discussion about the Diamond Jubilee and much praise for one's long and steady hand on the wheel of world politics. Mr Cameron said he 'spoke for all . . .'. Unfortunately we never got to hear exactly what he spoke for all for, mainly due to the DoE interrupting by shouting 'Cameron speaks for sod all' half way through.

Changed into something regal and jumped in the Bentley for the Commonwealth Day service at Westminster Abbey. It's one's annual opportunity to thank God for blessing one with the most beautiful countries in the world to rule and to thank him for omitting Denmark.

Had the various Commonwealth High Commissioners over to the Palace in the afternoon for tea, cupcakes in the shape of gin bottles and a game of 'Guess the Intro', which was won by the New Zealanders.

Friday 16th March 2012

One was looking forward to a Friday off when Dumbledore (the Archbishop of Canterbury) called to say he'd received his divine P45 from above and would be stepping down at the end of the year. Bollocks. One hates recruiting Archbishops of Canterbury. At least with Prime Ministers one can leave the decision to the public. Told him that the Lord and his Queen were grateful for his dedicated service and promised him a good reference and a leaving party.

Poured oneself a Holy Water (gin) and drafted a quick job advert. The Pope called to say he was interested in the vacancy and would pop his CV in the post, and Mr Clegg texted to enquire if he were Deputy Archbishop. The DoE replied pointing out that he was 'Deputy of Sod all', to which he didn't respond. Thought for a moment that Lambeth Palace had adopted the Catholic Pope style of selecting a new Church leader when one saw huge clouds of smoke floating down The Mall but it turns out they were coming from Clarence House and Camilla's mid-morning fag.

Mrs 'honestly, everyone calls me Carole' Middleton called to offer one her condolences on the resignation of the Archbishop. She'd apparently had the same trouble at their local church but said the new man was very nice and even did animal funerals.

SUNDAY 18TH MARCH 2012 – MOTHER'S DAY
Mother's Day. Awoke to find the children, grandchildren and great-grandchildren all gathered around one's bed with cards and

flowers, which was a little disconcerting at first. One thought Michael Fagan had returned and brought his relatives with him.

The DoE cooked up a round of boiled eggs and soldiers (not real soldiers) and we all sat around on one's bed whilst one opened one's cards and presents.

Catherine had knitted one a bed-throw with a huge crown and the words 'Sixty Years as the World's Mum' across it, which was nice. She said Mrs Middleton had donated the wool from her new mail order knitwear business. Right on cue, Mrs 'Really it's been almost a year, do call me Carole' Middleton called to say Happy Mother's Day 'from one mum to another'.

Popped down to the post room to read a selection of the 78million cards that had arrived. Mr Clegg text to say he would pop his in later, just as soon as the Pritt Stick dried as he didn't want to get glitter on his jumper.

Camilla, Anne, Catherine, Sophie, Zara, Autumn, Beatrice and Eugenie and I went for a girls walk in the afternoon with the corgis along the long walk and popped into Fudge Kitchen on the way back to the castle to pick up some presents for the boys. Bumped into some locals who remarked that we could make a fortune as Royal Family look-alikes. Worth some thought.

Back to the Castle to join the boys for afternoon tea and fudge. Catherine said the tea got cold awfully quickly and suggested to knit a tea-cosy to bring next time she visited. One does wonder if that girl has too much time on her hands up there in the arse-end of Wales.

TUESDAY 20TH MARCH 2012
Speech day at Parliament. One likes to address the muppets at Jubilee time. Queen Victoria had the Lords and MPs round to the Palace for her Diamond Jubilee address but one simply cannot have all those expense-dodgers eyeing up one's antique furniture, so one's off with the DoE to

Westminster Hall. Taking the State Bentley and a load of State Trumpeters to remind them who's in charge.

2pm: Well, that was traumatic. Honestly, addressing MPs is like dropping a stone into a well and never hearing a splash. Cameron, Clegg and Miliband sat there gazing and smiling like some kind of *Last of the Summer Wine* prequel and John Bercow, who is possibly the shortest politician one has ever met, delivered a rambling speech about one being a 'Kaleidoscope Queen'. Still, they'd all clubbed together to buy one a Diamond Jubilee present: a stained glass window. A stained glass sodding window. And one can't even take it home – they're keeping it at Westminster. What part of 'crate of gin' did they not understand? One's been dropping hints for months. One nodded and smiled and tried to make an early exit when the DoE and I got stuck in a lift. As if one hadn't spent enough time with one's elected masses. Finally made it back to the Palace for a well-deserved gin and tonic with almost no tonic.

Banana Man (George Osborne) popped round in the evening to run one through tomorrow's budget. He says there is nothing he can do about gin duty but promised to phase out the top rate of tax to compensate. One unfortunately didn't hear all the details, partly because one had him escorted off the premises before he'd finished so one could watch the new series of *Big Fat Gypsy Weddings*.

FRIDAY 6TH APRIL 2012 – GOOD FRIDAY

Arrived back at Windsor Castle last night and was up early for a Good Friday walk with the corgis this morning. Easter is one's favourite time of the year. It's little wonder they call it Good Friday. Popped in on one's Estate Manager on the way back to the Castle. He doesn't like to gossip but apparently one of one's chauffeurs is 'having it away' with a kitchen maid. We spent about three hours trying to figure out exactly who but unfortunately one had to rush off and rule in Jamaica for a few hours before supper.

Settled down in the evening to 'Midsomer
Murders' and an unconstitutionally large glass of
sweet sherry. Barnaby was just about to reveal
the murderer when Catherine called to say she
was knitting an Easter Bunny for Edward and
wanted to know what his favourite colour was
for the waistcoat. She didn't have any pink
unfortunately so decided to do it in purple instead.

Saturday 7th April 2012

Very excited. The Diamond Jubilee Royal Barge
is ready! One's having a flotilla pageant on the
Thames to celebrate one's sixty years on the
throne and one shall be front and centre on
the barge. Seriously considering sailing onto the
continent and firing a few warning shots at
the Europeans.

Trying to play the whole thing down, actually.
The Spanish in particular have been very
nervous at the sight of amassed British ships
since 1588 and the French have never recovered
from Waterloo in 1815. You might have thought

that people would learn not to sod around when the British are afloat but that didn't stop the Argies in 1982.

Having a hot crossed bun for elevenses and then off to inspect the barge.

7pm: Well. It's not the Royal Yacht Britannia, let's put it like that. The DoE said it looked more like a floating portaloo. Really, one cannot be seen floating down the Thames on that, one shall be an international laughing stock.

Got Zippy and Bungle (Mr Cameron and Boris Johnson) on a conference call and ran them through just how much additional gold was required to transform the barge into someone one could quite happily be seen reigning on. Mr Cameron said he 'felt confident' that he could find the funds to make the necessary changes. One said one 'felt confident' that one could call a general election if not. Was just about to hang up when George (Mr Clegg) completed the

Rainbow team by piping up that he had a remote controlled boat and asking if it would be any help at all. The DoE explained in graphic detail where his remote control would be most use and they all promptly disappeared to raid the Parliamentary Piggy Bank.

Camilla arrived at about 9pm with enough gin to launch a barge on and we spent the rest of the evening considering what an odd bunch politicians are.

Sunday 8th April 2012

Woke up in the Waterloo Chamber at Windsor Castle with Camilla. Not entirely sure how we ended up there, but at least we were on the floor and not swinging from a chandelier, which is more than could be said for Prince Andrew. Had a few footmen pick up Camilla and returned to one's private sitting room for a bacon sandwich and a pot of strong coffee. Uneasy lies the head that wears a crown this morning.

One was just starting to come to terms with life when the largest rabbit one has ever seen walked in wearing a bright purple waistcoat. Made a mental note to stay off the gin for a while before spotting Catherine behind it. Really, there is nothing that girl won't knit. She hopped off to give it to Edward and one jumped in the Bentley for the short ride down the hill to St George's Chapel for the Sunday service.

Back to the Royal Apartments for a late lunch and a hair of the corgi sherry.

MONDAY 9TH APRIL 2012 – EASTER MONDAY
We all gathered in the breakfast room for the traditional Easter Monday breakfast. Catherine had laid a place for the knitted Easter Bunny, which was nice. Spent the entire breakfast looking across at it and couldn't quite put ones finger on what had changed until it reached out for a piece of toast and one realised that it wasn't the knitted bunny but Edward who'd taken such

a shine to the waistcoat that he'd put it on himself. Catherine said if she'd have known she'd simply have knitted Edward a few new jumpers but he said the fluffy tail was his favourite bit, although the DoE was quite insistent that he couldn't wear it to church.

William was away on his helicopter but he'd sent Catherine an enormous Easter Egg filled with flowers. She said it was the most amazing thing she'd ever seen and promptly disappeared upstairs to knit something to keep it in.

Off to Church for the Easter Service. Stopped outside to accept flowers from some local school children. One gave them a bag of mini chocolate eggs and settled down to the Dean of Windsor's sermon, which he'd thankfully cut short by about two hours.

Easter-themed fancy dress party in the evening. Edward came as a knitted rabbit, obviously. Camilla came as a giant Easter Egg but did such a good job that she couldn't move and spent all evening in the corner of the Ballroom until one of the corgis started licking her legs.

Monday 7th May 2012 – Bank Holiday Monday

Bank Holiday Monday so one's staying at Windsor. Having the Olympic Organising Committee round to update one on the plans for the games (or 'Post-Jubilee Sports Days', as they are known in the Royal Household).

Lord Coe said he wanted to say a few words by way of introduction and was still going on about two hours later. Really should have never lorded that man. Explained in not insignificant detail that his continuing status as a peer was directly linked to the number of gold medals Britain achieved.

Apparently there's an acute shortage of hotel accommodation for visitors. Charles wondered if we could turn Buckingham Palace into some kind of youth hostel for a couple of months. Thankfully no one on the Olympic Organising Committee heard him, mainly because one had locked him outside. Still, he likes looking through the window at the grown ups talking. Finally agreed to let them use Windsor Great Park as a campsite on the strict understanding that no campfires are allowed – we've seen enough flames at Windsor to last a lifetime. Edward burst in shouting 'did someone say camp?!', which was rather awkward, to say the least.

Apparently the cyclists are one's best bet for a gold this year. Boris Johnson says he's hoping they'll inspire a new generation of London cyclists, which might go some way to explain why he's cluttered up the streets of one's capital with bright blue cycle lanes and 'Boris bikes'.

Had a quick run through of the opening ceremony arrangements, which shall be called 'Islands of Wonder'. One wanted to call it 'The

Empire Strikes Back' but it was generally felt that might intimidate some of the smaller nations.

Sunday 13th May 2012 – The Diamond Jubilee Pageant, Windsor Castle

Up early with the corgis for a wander down to the showground in one's garden at Windsor to see how preparations for this evening's Diamond Jubilee Pageant are coming along. They've had a couple of dress rehearsals over the last few days but tonight is the main event, mainly because one shall be attending personally.

It's all looking rather serious. They wanted to represent the different countries one has during one's reign and the variety of cultures across the Commonwealth. The DoE says he would have been happy with a quick PowerPoint presentation but they wanted to make a bit more effort apparently.

Horses seem to be the name of the games,
and quite frankly one has never seen so many
amassed in one place. The Cavalry Regiment,
Royal Horse Artillery and The Household
Cavalry are here in case any of the foreign
visitors get out of hand.

Wished them well and retreated to the Castle for
a Jubilee Pageant of custard creams.

11pm: Well. That was quite an experience. No
one mentioned the Kremlin Mounted Cossacks
had been invited. The Duchess of Cornwall nearly
leapt out of her chair, poor thing. Charles said she
hasn't looked that worried since being poked with
a stick during last year's London riots. Thankfully
the Royal Canadian Mounted Police got them
under control without the need for more substan-
tial British force and calm was restored by the
time the Cook Island Dancers turned up. They
don't have any armed forces in the Cook Islands,
preferring instead to repel foreign aggressors with
the most camp dancing one has ever seen.

The show finished with South African Zulu Warriors, who looked like one of Prince Harry's fancy dress parties, and one was safely back behind the walls of the castle and in bed by midnight.

Friday 1st June 2012 – Diamond Jubilee Weekend

Bloody hell, is Gary Barlow still here?! One really cannot wait until Monday's concert is over and done with. If one sees that man walking around with a tape measure and clipboard one more time one might get quite unconstitutionally rude. Still, to be fair he's done a lovely job on the stage. Who knew he was so good with his hands. The DoE says it's amazing what you can do with a bit of 2x4 and a good saw.

Spent the day dealing with matters of global political importance and settled down in the evening with a gin and tonic of 'Diamond Jubilee' proportions. There are already people gathering outside the Palace, which in many parts of the world would bring about panic in a Head of State.

It all kicks off in the morning. Look at one's diary:

Saturday: Epsom Derby (Take cash. Not Euros)
Sunday: Take Royal Barge down the Thames for Diamond Jubilee Pageant
Monday: Gary Barlow's little concert outside the Palace (take iPod with Led Zeppelin, Queen and Foo Fighters playlist). Light national Diamond Jubilee beacon (take Camilla's lighter)
Tuesday: Service of Thanksgiving and carriage procession from St. Paul's (smile and nod, smile and nod)

So, this is it. The Diamond Jubilee. One wonders who the next monarch to celebrate sixty years on the throne will be. And what kind of a world they will reign over.

So much has changed. And yet so much remains the same.

This royal throne of kings, this sceptred isle,
This earth of majesty, this seat of Mars,
This other Eden, demi-paradise,
This fortress built by Nature for herself
Against infection and the hand of war,
This happy breed of men, this little world,
This precious stone set in the silver sea,
Which serves it in the office of a wall
Or as a moat defensive to a house,
Against the envy of less happier lands,
This blessed plot, this earth, this realm, this
England.

Looked back at Queen Victoria's diary from
1897. There are only a few words written on
the eve of her diamond jubilee: 'Gin O'Clock'.
Goodness, look at the time.

The Diamond Jubilee Martini

Three parts gin
One part gin
Dash of gin
Twist of lemon

Her Majesty's Sent Items

From: EIIR
To: The PM
Subject: This afternoon's audience

Dear Prime Minister,

One is very much looking forward to this afternoon's audience and to hearing all about your little adventures. Unfortunately, due to having to rule in approximately fifteen other sovereign nations, one may have to cut your time short by twenty five minutes. Will five minutes be enough to cover everything? As suggested, one has made a few cuts at the Palace, starting with your chair, so you may want to bring one with you.

As ever, your loving and gracious Queen,

EIIR

From: EIIR
To: William
Subject: The Middletons

William, dear,

One really is persevering with the Middletons,
but they were at Ascot today placing £2.50 each-
way bets and frankly it was a bit awkward for all
concerned. One's bookmaker didn't know where
to look. We can't expect the poor man to take
the Solomon Islands on the nose in the 2.15 one
minute and then to be giving 'change for a fiver'
the next. And one really doesn't need any more
mail order party plates, union flag design or not.
Can you have a word?

Hope Canada is fun. Go careful in the French-
speaking bits, they're very sensitive.

Granny

From: EIIR

To: Deputy PM

Subject: Have you done anything?

Mr Clegg,

What have you done? Have you done anything?

EIIR

From: EIIR

To: Rebekah Brooks, News International

Subject: Voicemails

Mrs Brooks,

The DoE has misplaced his voicemail PIN. One wonders if you might let him know if he has any urgent messages?

EIIR

From: EIIR

To: HH The Pope

Subject: Beatification of Freddie Mercury

Your Holiness,

Further to our discussion regarding the potential beatification of Freddie Mercury, one wonders if you have made any progress? As you know, one was most keen for full sainthood to be attained in time for one's Diamond Jubilee in 2012. Your office have asked for evidence of miracles performed by Mr Mercury and one's private secretary has sent copies of Queen's *The Miracle* album and a DVD of their Live Aid performance from 1985. Might one also point you in the direction of the 'Bohemian Rhapsody' video?

One has written to the Archbishop of Canterbury to suggest an equivalent spiritual recognition in the Church of England, but until that time, and as Defender of the Faith, one really must insist that some progress is made on this issue in Rome.

EIIR

From: EIIR
To: Tony Blair
Subject: Your memoirs

Mr Blair,

Thank you so much for sending a copy of your memoirs. One found them to be a most entertaining read, which really is testament to your writing as one is not usually a fan of fiction. You'll be pleased to know that they have taken a very important place in the Royal Library, propping open the door. Unfortunately, your former communications director's memoirs didn't survive the DoE's Bonfire Night Party, but one feels sure that these would have been an equally thrilling read.

EIIR

From: EIIR

To: Lord Mingen-Jones

Subject: RE: I think the PM's gone mad

My Lord, yes, one is urgently looking into this.

EIIR

From: EIIR

To: The Leader of the Opposition

Subject: RE: My party doesn't know who I am

Dear Mr Miliband,

Thank you for your note regarding your problems getting people in your party to recognise you. One really wouldn't worry; no one else in the country recognises you either.

As ever, your loving Queen,

EIIR

From: EIIR

To: The Keeper of the Royal Diaries

Subject: Might publish a book

Mr Pumpkin-Smyth,

Could you find out one's diaries from the last year? One is considering publishing some extracts in a book. Might call it *Gin O'Clock*.

EIIR

From: EIIR

To: David Cameron and Boris Johnson

Subject: The Barge

What part of 'majestic' do you two not understand? Have you actually seen it? One is simply not floating down the Thames on a glorified canal boat. It doesn't even have a state dining room, for Christ's sake. You've got about three weeks to transform it into something that looks a bit more like the Royal Yacht Britannia or one will be sailing down to Westminster to call a general election.

DRAFT OF QUEEN'S

CHRISTMAS MESSAGE

I address you now, as your ever-loving Queen, Defender of the Faith and Supreme Governor of the Church of England at this, most special, time of the year. Christmas is a time for families; for quiet contemplation of the year that has passed and for looking forward to the year ahead. It is a time when we are reminded that, no matter what difficulties we face in our daily lives, there are almost always people worse off than us, and they are usually French, Greek or Spanish.

The Duke of Edinburgh and I look back with affection on the Eurovision Song Contest in May, when we were reminded how very strange our European neighbours really are. It is these special moments in our lives that remind us why the United Kingdom is physically and emotionally separate from Europe. Music, of course, is an international language that we may all speak and from which we may all learn. At this year's Eurovision Song Contest, we learned that Estonia has deep-rooted social problems, that Greece has never fully recovered from the loss of its monarchy and that the Moldavians have exceptionally pointy heads. We also noted that things are obviously very difficult in Austria.

Also in May, we welcomed President and Mrs Obama for their first State Visit to the United Kingdom. I was delighted to seal the very special bond between our countries, crystallised by the enduring probation on which one has placed this most difficult colony. We are reminded that we share a common language, which over the last two centuries the Americans have taken and ruined. I hope that my meetings with President Obama may go some way towards putting this right.

The Americans have, of course, contributed much to the United Kingdom and our way of life, and for many people this is felt most in the iPhone. As we look forward to the coming years, we hope that one day the advances of technology will allow us to use this wonderful device to make calls, even in one's Highland residence.

The Duke of Edinburgh and I were delighted to make our first visit to the Republic of Ireland, having purchased it during the banking crisis. This simple act of friendship between nations shows that there is nothing that cannot be achieved by a loving and gracious Queen. And one was especially delighted to have agreed the historic treaty that brought an end to Bono as a legal entity. I know the whole nation will join with the Duke of Edinburgh and me in rejoicing at never again having to listen to this man's self-righteous outpourings.

Of course, this year has not been without its trials and tribulations. It has been a particularly testing time for the media, politicians and the police, all of whom have been found to be horribly interdependent and seriously wanting. It is at times such as these that I say to you: trust no one but yourself and your Queen.

As we sit down to our Christmas dinners, there are many of our brave men and women of the armed forces putting British military might to good use policing the world and keeping scoundrels, villains, dictators and the French at bay. We are all more secure thanks to the sacrifices they make, and I salute their dedication and bravery in the name of Queen and country.

Most of all, Christmas is a time for children, and I draw particular pleasure from seeing them develop and grow. Mr Clegg has shown himself to be something of an artist and there is no doubt that his drawings have brightened up the walls of the Downing Street Cabinet Room. I was also thrilled to learn that Mr Osborne is finally getting to grips with counting and can now count to twenty using both hands and both feet. I very much hope that by the end of next year Mr Miliband may have learned to speak in fully formed sentences.

It is also a time for loved ones. This year, we celebrated ninety years of the Duke of Edinburgh. In his long and dedicated service to this country and to the Commonwealth, there is not a corner of the earth that he has not offended, not an animal that he has not shot, not a politician who he hasn't berated and not a curse that he hasn't uttered. He has also, of course, brought happiness, hope and aspiration to many hundreds of thousands of young people through the Duke of Edinburgh's Awards Scheme, and to many millions of people through the charities and causes he champions so tirelessly. He has, through these many years, been my liegeman and greatest comfort, inspiration and support. My DoE. We owe him a great debt of gratitude.

Of course, the year also saw the marriage of one's granddaughter, Zara Phillips to that Rugby chap and that of Prince William and Catherine, the new Duke and Duchess of Cambridge. That day represented more than a marriage. It represented the coming together of two families, and I am pleased that Mr and Mrs Middleton's respective families were able to use the event to this end.

It was also a very personal opportunity for the Duke of Edinburgh and oneself to renew the bonds with Royal Families from throughout Europe. We will remember with great affection King Simeon II of Bulgaria's superlative breakfast and the Crown Prince of the Netherlands' evening performance, which, while unorthodox to say the least, brought a smile to Prince Edward's face. We were, of course, all delighted that such a happy day for William and Catherine also saw the blossoming of love between the Queen of Spain and Phillip Schofield.

2012 will doubtlessly bring with it its own opportunities and challenges. Particularly sporty people look forward to the Olympic Games in London, and many, many more look forward to one's Diamond Jubilee celebrations throughout the Commonwealth.

William and Catherine's first overseas tour of Canada reminded us all that the world needs Royal leadership more than ever, and the many thousands of people who turned out to greet them attest to the enduring spirit of monarchy felt across all continents. In the face of incompetent politicians, reckless bankers and amoral phone hackers the world over, one assures you all that your Queen loves you and, in the words of the great British poet, Freddie Mercury, 'talent will out, my dear'.

I wish you and those whom you love and care for a very happy Christmas. God Save One.

Royal Acknowledgements

One should like to thank one's many hundreds of thousands of Twitter followers past and present and, in particular, one's literary agent and principal Canadian subject, Dame Sarah Williams GVCO at Royal Ed Victor for suggesting that one publish these extracts from the Royal Diaries. One should also like to thank one's editor, Dame Fenella Bates GCB, and everyone at Royal Hodder and Stoughton, Publishers by Appointment.

And, of course, the Royal Family, and one's two little princesses in particular.

But most of all, one should like to thank the gracious, majestic and loving Queen Elizabeth II. Long may She reign.

Twitter.com/@Queen_UK
facebook.com/royalginoclock